P9-CKR-073

SURVIVAL OF THE THICKEST

SURVIVAL OF THE THICKEST

ESSAYS

MICHELLE BUTEAU

GALLERY BOOKS

New York   London   Toronto   Sydney   New Delhi

Gallery Books
An Imprint of Simon & Schuster, Inc.
1230 Avenue of the Americas
New York, NY 10020

Copyright © 2020 by Michelle Buteau

Certain names have been changed.

All rights reserved, including the right to reproduce this book
or portions thereof in any form whatsoever. For information,
address Gallery Books Subsidiary Rights Department,
1230 Avenue of the Americas, New York, NY 10020.

First Gallery Books hardcover edition December 2020

GALLERY BOOKS and colophon are registered trademarks of
Simon & Schuster, Inc.

For information about special discounts for bulk purchases,
please contact Simon & Schuster Special Sales at 1-866-506-1949
or business@simonandschuster.com.

The Simon & Schuster Speakers Bureau can bring authors to your
live event. For more information or to book an event, contact the
Simon & Schuster Speakers Bureau at 1-866-248-3049 or
visit our website at www.simonspeakers.com.

Interior design by A. Kathryn Barrett

Manufactured in the United States of America

10 9 8 7 6 5 4 3 2 1

Library of Congress Cataloging-in-Publication Data is available.

ISBN 978-1-9821-2258-4
ISBN 978-1-9821-2260-7 (ebook)

to gijs aka bob. you're my first, the last, my everything.

Contents

SURVIVAL OF THE **THICKEST**

JERSEY STRONG

Jersey. The state and its people bring a lot of things to mind. When you think of Jerseyans, you might think of loud, brash people in leopard-skin clothing with red-painted lips and big hair. If that's what you picture: you're absolutely right. No shade to Jersey, but there's a reason why *The Sopranos* and *Jersey Shore* were big-assed hits. We a mess. Whether you're Black, brown, white, or in between, we're gonna meet you at our closest Wawa, cop a hoagie, get that extra red sauce on the side at that I-talian place, drive "down the shore" just so we can yell at someone to drive properly, but not before yelling at someone else to *not* fuck up our sneakers. (Dude, they brand-new.) Jerseyites are a yelly people. Get used to it. We're also the state with the most diners per capita and we're the spot where that jackass Aaron Burr killed Alexander Hamilton, kicking off a whole musical and a bunch of other shit.

There are a few states that feel like a nationality. Jersey is one of them. We're supposed to be the Garden State, but "Fuggedaboutit!" is really the people's slogan, and never mind my position as to where the Statue of Liberty really resides. (It's in Jersey, bitches!) I was born in North Jersey, raised in Central Jersey, and spent my last year in South Jersey, right outside of Philly. Shit, I've seen it all! I'm like the Jersey Khaleesi, but my Drogo was a guy from Trenton who wore a Naughty by Nature T-shirt with Karl Kani jeans. No matter where I lived in the Dirty Jerz, my neighborhood was always predominantly Italians and Irish. If you were Polish, then you were exotic. I mean, so many letters in your last name—how does it even fit on an ID? There was also a smattering of Chinese, Indian, and Arab families, but they mostly stuck together. Samesies for the Black folks. Then there was my family. The light-skinned Caribbean folks all willy-nilly on the wrong side of the tracks having it out with the Italians and Irish just trying to make shit work. It did not work. We were always the odd men out. We were the light-skinned family no one could quite put a finger on. We were the white sheep, with weird accents, exotic food, and loud music no one's ever heard of. We were the "Bob Marley Family" because that's the closest thing anyone could compare us to. Yes, you got that right. My childhood was all "No Woman, No Cry" whether I liked it or not. Here's a typical rundown of an interaction from my childhood with another Jerseyan:

They: What are you?

Me: Human.

They: Are you Black?

4

Me: Yes, that okay?

They: What do you consider yourself?

Me: Cute.

They: Who's white in your family though?

Me: Who sent you, Hitler?

I don't know why everyone in Jersey becomes a representative for 23andMe when it comes to a light-skinned face that doesn't speak Spanish. But they sure do. If you're a light-skinned Black person that's not Puerto Rican people lose their gahtdamn minds. If someone speaks Spanish to you and you say, "Sorry, I don't speak Spanish," they look at you like they just met a short guy whose license says he's six foot four. I would tell people I was Jamaican and Haitian, and they would looked confused as fuck. There was even that time when somebody said to me, "Well, then, shouldn't you be darker with a basket of fruit on your head?" And that was my guidance counselor—bitch, please. The parents of my friends would say shit like, "But you don't look Jamaican *or* Haitian." Really? Have you been there? No? Then shut up.

My father was born and raised in Les Cayes, Haiti. His mother raised him with her sisters. She was a twin. She had brown skin, and her sisters had dark skin. My grandma had had a relationship with a man; those are the only details I know. Shit, I don't even know if my dad has a birth certificate. But my grandma got pregnant, and legend has it (please don't get me started on deep-rooted Caribbean-family secrets) they couldn't be together because she had darker skin than him.

So she just went off and did her thing and raised my dad. His father went off and married someone with light skin and had a whole other family. The resemblance between the two families is frightening. In the case of the Haitian doctor and the nurse?! Yes, you are the son! Evidence? Just look in the fucken' mirror! My father never grew up with a dad, yet he was a pretty great dad for me growing up. I mean, yeah, he's batshit crazy and hot-tempered, but he's human as fuck.

My grandfather had a lot of children, kind of like a Mormon dude but without the compound. So it's hard to say how many people I am actually related to. To give you an example of how this plays out, my friends will have strangers slide into their DMs to say "u cute" or "u up?" But for me, strangers slide into my DMs to be like: "I think we're cousins? No, really, I think we're related." Holidays are always so easy! JK. LOLz. They're not. My mother is from Jamaica and has four brothers between her two parents. Truly, she's a loyal sister and a selfless wife. She's also a pretty solid mom, except for her snooping problem. Momsies is like a real-life CSI, wearing blazers, crunching numbers, inspecting the suspicious toothpaste left around the sink, and reading my diary. Yep, I had a diary when I was ten, and she read that shit and then chicken-breast grilled me on it. She was like, "Why didn't you tell me you have a crush on a guy named Russell?" That's why, to this day, I can't remember shit and I never write anything down. (Because what you don't remember, you don't really know. Just ask that white girl from *Home-*

6

land.) If I had to diagnose it, I'd say I have Jamaican-mom PTSD. Whenever I hear my little firecracker of a mom coming around any corner (even now) starting in with that disapproving accent, I duck and cover and then point at my sibling, which is weird because I'm an only child. It just goes to show you, deflect and defend is a great domestic policy in my little world. I stand by it. I truly do.

So, back to Jersey. The first house my parents ever owned was a cute, starter-kit home in a blue-collar neighborhood with a sunken living room, sunroom, and one bathroom. If you know me, then you know my dream home is going to have at least five bedrooms and twenty-seven bathrooms. Having so many toilets that no one in the house knows what kind of day you've had? Now, that's a true sign of success. We also had a big backyard and Jah bless my parents, they didn't know they had purchased a house in a flood zone. Ain't that cute? My earliest and first childhood memories will forever be around what I call "THE FLOODS." I remember my neighbor was in her driveway in a canoe rowing down the street like it was another normal day in Jersey. But, hey, that shit looked fun. So I joined in. What other light-skinned girl can say she learned how to swim in her driveway? I don't know another one. Do you? Well, then we're probably related. Give her my number.

Our neighbors had a daughter named Jen who is one of my oldest friends; we still keep in touch to this day. Our moms were knocked up at the same time together. Jen was

7

born exactly thirty days before me. So we were destined to be friends. Plus, our moms were probably throwing off some mad pheromones at each other from across the driveways separating our houses. I can only imagine the vortex of juju that created. Seriously, though, ain't that the real reason people love their neighbors? They go through some real, intense life shit together, like another human being kicking out of your undercarriage to carve out her place in the world. Jen had two older brothers, and I was an only child, and we hung tough. Truth be told, we shared everything like sisters. My dad would take me around the block on the back of his bike. Then he'd come back, take me off, put Jen on the bike, and take her around too. We tried out together for the school play in our Catholic grammar school, and neither of us made the cut. But the nuns felt bad so they put us in some Old Testament production about the beginning of creation. I had to wear a black leotard, and Jen had to wear a white one. I was supposed to play the "darkness," and she was supposed to play the "light." It took me years to realize that shit was racist as fuck. When we weren't at school, we watched movies together like *Ya-Ya Sisterhood of the Traveling Pants* and *Beaches*. Jen was a type of friend on *Dawson's Creek* but in real life. Ya know the type. The kind of friend that helps you tuck old clothes into your bed so it looks like you're still sleeping there, and meanwhile you sneak out. Maybe you head down to the river to throw rocks in it while you walk around and talk about what you're gonna be when you grow up, maybe stumble across a dead body. Jen was that bish. My OG. My Fisher-Price ride-or-die.

Now, even close friendships have their reasons for shifting into something else. People grow up; they grow apart. It's normal and even healthy. With Jen, that started with her Madonna collection. She was so obsessed with Madonna. (Not the Catholic one, the one now in her sixties who still rides horses, talks in a British accent, had sex with her trainer, and, oh yeah, sings?) Now look, I had a Michael Jackson obsession too. (And of course that shit has been #canceled. Permanently. Due to the fact that he did those terrible things— yes, he did. Open your eyes, people.) But at the time, my MJ mania felt like just the right amount of childhood, celebrity fangirl-ness without being in the cray-cray zone. Jen's obsession, though, was next level. You could never say anything sideways about Madonna. She'd get so mad and take it all personal. When she did that, I was always like, "Bish, you think Madonna cares about you?" And I mean, I knew this at, like, five years old.

I knew this adult years later who had a Tweety Bird collection. There were literally Tweety Birds all over her damn apartment. She had Tweety Bird posters, a wallet, Tweety Bird earrings, socks, car trinkets, mugs, *et mas*. It was wild. And that's the thing: When someone obsesses like that into adulthood, you're thinking, *Where's the Tweety Bird kill room? I know she got bodies somewhere around here stuffed into Tweety Bird slankets and surrounded by all this Tweety*

Bird propaganda. All I could think was, *Oh, I knew this was the wrong place to get a flat tire! I've seen* Misery! *I need my kneecaps, huney!* With Jen, it was like that. She had that Madonna obsession into her damn forties. I know I'm supposed to be coming from a place of love on this one, but I cannot. Your development has been arrested. In fact, it has been handcuffed and thrown into a pop culture remix of *Intervention*! If you're going to complain that no one takes you seriously, you gotta dress for the job that you want, and that might mean leaving your hundred rubber bracelets and lace dress at home! I don't know why this affects me so much. Making one person your end-all-be-all nationality feels cultish. Jen is so much more than knowing every lyric to every Madonna song ever made, but this is who she is, and I have to love her no matter what. She's a real one, sister, and daughter, no matter the fuck what. Madonna, if you're reading this, can you do us all a damn favor and shout out this lovely human being I've known for all time so I don't have to talk about it anymore?

Black to Jersey . . . my parents and I moved from house to house and eventually ended up in a suburb of Parsippany. The next house I remember was bigger and not that far from the first, but in a better neighborhood because my dad got a promotion. It had a circular driveway, and there were zero kids around to play with. So I learned to play duets on the piano by myself, and I developed a really good imagination because that's what you do when you're an only child and your dad moves you to a neighborhood of old-assed white ladies. But at least these Golden Girls got Entenmann's, so I grabbed a piece of crumb cake to eat on the lanai and made the best of it.

My dad told me his favorite memory of this particular house was listening to me struggle outside as I tried to teach myself how to ride my bike. (Um, here's an idea . . . help me, then?) By the time he made it out into the yard to see what I was doing, I had already figured it all out and was pedaling down the block. He is still dead proud of that. I don't remember this shit at all. Instead, I imagine we had some kind of *This Is Us* moment where my dad is chasing me down a tree-lined block with one hand on the back of my bike trying to help me find my balance. I eventually get it and ride away, as my dad yells, "You got this, Michelle! Go! That's it!" That is not how the man does shit at all.

There was this one time when I was about fifteen and my father said to me, "Stop eating pasta in front of your boyfriend, and you should lose twenty pounds because then you'd be so beautiful."

I stopped right there. I told him off. I said, "I am beautiful no matter what, twenty pounds or not. And if someone is going to love me, they are going to love me for me."

His look changed immediately and he said, "That's my girl!"

Uh-huh, yeah, wasn't there a better way to get that outta me? But that's my dad. He always had a warped way of showing me I could be strong. When I was seven, he had me follow him around the yard to bag up all the leaves he was cutting off the tree. For each bag I collected, he gave me a dollar, but I was seven and that shit was hard. So I said to him, "Hold up, you're violating child labor laws, and slow down." My dad laughed so hard, he still talks about it.

Then there was the time I did some kind of nonsense I can't remember in the car when I was real young and my dad lost his temper and yelled, "Stupid little bitch!" He felt really bad about it when he calmed down. I know because he gave me this cuckoo clock afterwards. Now to this day, I hate muthafuckin' cuckoo clocks. As an adult, I had this therapist with a wall full of cuckoo clocks. I kid you not. Our time would be up, and the wall full of cuckoos would "cuckoo-cuckoo" with the little birds popping out of the clocks. I almost burned that place down. It was like in *Sleeping with the Enemy* when Julia Roberts's character comes home and sees the damn cans have been, like, OCD rearranged by her psycho ex-husband. But I was the psycho ex, and the cans were the cuckoo clocks, and I was going to ring all their little birdie necks at once while screaming "Red rum!" So run, bitch, run. You see what therapy does? It makes you learn things about yourself. Yep, my dad had a next-level temper. No doubt about it. But he never laid a hand on us. It was mostly just loud and at times a little cuckoo. (See what I did there?)

He also thought really highly of himself, my dad, which

I've grown to appreciate. I mean, to give you a visual, this man would walk around in a red polo shirt with some curly chest hair popping out of his gold chains like taco meat, some tight-assed white shorts like a pro tennis instructor, a Jheri curl when he didn't have a full-on Afro, and some black sunglasses. Always black sunglasses. I honestly don't think I ever saw my dad's eyes until I was a teenager. I would beg him to take these sunglasses off, at least for school trips, but he never did. I guess it upped my cache, though, because for years the other kids thought he was my security. And when it rained? My dad gave zero fucks. He'd be looking all dapper in a three-piece suit and then he'd straight up put a shower cap on his Afro. I've seen this man put a plastic ShopRite bag around his S-curl. It was always the perfect combo of classy and gully. He also speaks eight languages, can cook better than my mom, and can dance like he's one of those instructors doing a foxtrot into a merengue with a dip on *Dancing with the Stars*. In his spare time, he made furniture on the side for the house. I don't know if he is cheap or a Renaissance man, but this is what Haitian dads are like: educated, proud, debonair, next level. He also named me after himself. That's right. I'm a Jr. I don't know if that's because he loves me or he's bad at remembering names, but I like to think the former. Merci beaucoup, Michel Buteau, *je t'aime*.

There was this one other time I'll tell you about regarding my dad. I was six years old and playing kickball with the other kids on the playground at my Catholic school. A quick word on Cathy (short for "Catholic") school. Everyone thinks they're sending their kids there to get a better education with some kind of moral direction. But the truth is, Cathy school can be just like public school or worse, and this particular day the playground felt like *Orange Is the New Black*, season one. It was a tense game of kickball, like really tense. These other six-year-olds were *Lord of the Flies* aggressive. I had been having a good game and was feeling ready to help bring home the sippy cup. I stepped up to kick the ball when this bully named Scott called me a nigger. He didn't say it like we were homies, he said that shit like Michael Richards having a bad set at the Laugh Factory. I was so young and so polite that I said, "Thank you!" and ran around the bases. But, full disclosure, I didn't even know what a nigger was. I had to ask this other little girl that I shared snacks with named Debbie. (I know, I shared my Little Debbie snacks with a little Debbie, *bienvenue à Neuva Jersey*.) Lil' Deb told me that it was a "bad Black person."

When I got home, I told my dad, and he said, "Congratulations, you're Black. Where's your lunch box? I'm not buying another lunch box." Then he helped me with my math homework and that was that. Zero fucks given. Message received.

JERSEY WRONG

In high school I had an Indian friend who was dating a Black guy, a Korean friend who was dating a light-skinned Black dude, and a Puerto Rican friend who was dating a Puerto Rican dude that she wanted to save herself for, and, wow, we were all doing the damn thing like a United Nations FUBU commercial. Yes, Jersey, we were out here representing. I felt like I had my crew even though there were still groups of people who didn't like me. But it was like *Fame* walking down the halls. I never felt so free. The Black girls that could sing, the Spanish girls that could dance, the Greek people who had curly hair. I'd walk down the hallway just taking in the diversity. And one fine-ass afternoon at the beginning of my freshman semester I had seen the most beautiful person. Ever. A tall, brown, black-haired, awkwardly lanky dude with clothes just swimming on him. I didn't know who he was, but I fell hard at first sight.

His name was Hakeem and he was from Central Asia. He was one of six kids, which is a small family for people where he's from. My friend introduced me to Hakeem, and I couldn't stop smiling. We were inseparable from day one, like an ethnic version of *The Notebook* without the Alzheimer's. I would always invite everyone in school to my house because I had a huge finished basement perfect for teenage angst and spin the bottle. The first time Hakeem came over we danced to Michael Jackson's "Remember the Time," which is pretty ironic that I'm remembering that time. His parents didn't speak English, but I was really into it. It was so long ago it almost feels like it never happened. I can't remember if he could dance. I can't remember if he was good at math. It's funny the things we do remember though. I remember he smoked cigarettes and had a warm smile. His nose was so big it touched his top lip. I thought it was the cutest thing I'd ever seen. He was my first kiss, and—okay, wow—yes, it was intense. His face smelled like smoke, and I thought that was very adult. He stuck his tongue in my mouth, and I immediately thought, *Interesting, I didn't know someone could lick your soul.* He held my face and slightly pinched my cheek after and said, "That was so great." I realized that I had stopped breathing and was like, "I think I love you; do you want some chicken my dad made?"

We were inseparable and dated almost all four years. There's nothing sweeter than having a cool boyfriend or girlfriend in high school. My parents liked him too. We weren't having sex because I was *très,* über Cathy and wanted to wait till I was married. I started getting brave and having Hakeem over right after school when my parents weren't home (this shit was forbidden as fuck), but I thought, *Whatever! I know my heart!*

We wouldn't do much, we'd just hang, make out, do homework, watch MTV. One day after eating leftover Jamaican food, Hakeem took it to the next level. He put his hands in my pants like it was the junk drawer in a kitchen and he was looking for tape to wrap a present. He whispered that I looked like Neneh Cherry and I was ready to marry him. I felt everything in my body jump, and I couldn't stop my nervous laughter covering my mouth. I was like Joaquin Phoenix in *Joker*, just a wild nervous laugh like a what-the-fuck.

I loved this boy more than all the poems, all the Romeos and Juliets, all the rom-coms. He was my first and last thought. When you're in high school, you're Bella in *Twilight*. The minute you find someone, it's like you're bound to them. I remember my mom was so nervous that I would convert to Islam. I'm not gonna lie, I was flirting with the idea. I went to a Muslim party one time with his family, and women were covering their hair and had beautiful full-length dresses on. In the Caribbean culture, it doesn't matter what you wear, it feels like you're a sex object. I was into the idea that I didn't have to do my hair (this was back in the day when I used to relax my hair and have it straightened, so you know I couldn't sweat or be caught in the rain). It was so strange walking up into the party, though, because there were two rooms: one with all the women, and the other with the men.

That was pretty wild for me. I didn't know that could be a thing. I wasn't mad at it; it felt like an adult slumber party. There's a conception that men are superior, but to be honest I didn't actually feel like the men were superior. When I learned that certain Muslim men could have up to four wives, I was like, *How is that possible? I'm way too jealous to do that shit. There's no way that that could go down.* Shit, if you asked me what I thought about that now in my forties? I'd say, "Please come over, sister wife. Let's fold this laundry. Please help me hold a baby, and, whatever, you can touch my husband's penis; I'm tired!"

Hakeem's parents opened a pizzeria, and they had a private blessing ceremony with family to slaughter a goat for good luck and prosperity. Growing up I'd go visit my grandma in Kingston for the summer, so I was used to butchered meat and goat parts everywhere. I'd play with a tied-up goat in the backyard, then all of a sudden they were gone and then we'd have soup for a week. I didn't think anything of it. So when my Muslim boyfriend told me that his parents were gonna kill this goat, I weirdly was like, "Okay! Cool. I'm game, lemme know if I can help." Um. Walking into this blessing was sort of like thinking you're totally prepared to go skydiving. I mean, yeah, you know what's gonna happen. You've been on a roller coaster before. But truly nothing could prepare you for what you will witness because it is burned in your brain forever and forever unless you vape the pain away, and now we can't do that anymore because vaping is like going down on a microwave. The goat was a baby goat, and everyone was speaking Arabic, so I was just trying to not make eye contact with the wrong person as a sign of disrespect, but as a curious American teenager my eyes were like the size of fucking quarters. They tied the goat up, said a prayer in Arabic, and then chopped its head off. "I'm so sorry, baby goat!" I silently whispered to myself over and over. The poor goat shit itself, they cleaned that up along with the blood pouring everywhere, turned it on its side, and sliced its body open for the contents. Everyone had a job, and they did it carefully. His sister removed the stomach and organs and went to the kitchen to clean it immediately. His mom soaked up the blood. His dad chopped the goat into limbs and other pieces as if this were second nature, and Hakeem and his brother carefully curated the limbs into bags, which then were brought to the kitchen. I just stood there in disbelief. I'm so sorry, baby goat. I didn't know what to do or how to make myself appear busy. Within minutes I was offered fried tripe. What a mixed bag of emotions. I know I'm a hypocrite, because I eat meat, but seeing it low-key butchered in front of you is a bit traumatizing. You forget that you're eating something that has been killed. It's just not a thing on your plate with sauce that magically shows up. But there was also something beautiful about this tradition that they all had together; there was something old-world about it. And that a goat could feed several families well was also heartening. It was moments like these that I loved Hakeem and being with him. We were both so different, but our love—albeit high school love—felt mature and real.

One of my best friends in high school was this thick-ass white girl named Denise; we called her Dee Dee for short. She had long brown hair, a small waist, and a bubble butt. Dee Dee was a bit of a spitfire—she smoked cigarettes (so bad!) and loved Puerto Rican dudes. Her and Hakeem never got along, and that was pretty annoying. Dee Dee was always getting into trouble and taking me down with her! She was the bad-influencer friend everybody had in school. One time she convinced me to call the school as my mother to say I was sick so she could come over and make out with her Puerto Rican boyfriend. What the fuck did I do that for? I'll never forget when her mom came over to get her from my house and pulled her out the door by her hair like it was a season finale of *Love & Hip Hop*. Her mom, with dark beady eyes, pointed at me and screamed, "You! You've made my daughter a nigger lover!" Yeah, that shit happened.

White folks loved using that word in my neighborhood. In today's climate you'd be canceled, fired, get an intervention, but not back then. We didn't have cameras on our phones to show the receipts. We didn't have Shaun King putting someone out there. We just had people that would say shit and then you'd have to get over it and still show up to the football game and sit next to them. Man. If only kids knew how good they have it today. If only Dee Dee's mom knew half the shit she was doing and that I was actually a good influence.

Then it was our junior year in high school. Hakeem and I were still going strong even though we were not engaged and we still hadn't had sex because I was waiting till we were married! Dee Dee and I were still friends, running around the mall drinking Slurpees, and she was still getting her bubble butt grounded. One night, out of nowhere, I had a weird dream that Dee Dee and Hakeem were bumping and grinding to that lame song "Lady in Red." I thought what a weird dream, but what was really weird was this undeniable gut feeling with absolutely no proof that they were hooking up. Or had hooked up? I don't know, but something didn't feel right; it felt off. Up until then it had always been: "Keep me away from her; she's awful." Or: "Ugh, you're with him tonight? Gross. Call me when you're free."

A couple of days later I was at the annual spring carnival hanging with Dee Dee and our Greek friend, Athena. I ordered a couple of rides on a Tilt-A-Whirl with Dee Dee and Athena. I remember being so nervous trying to work up the courage to tell her about my dream and low-key confront her. The ride went by so fast, truly a whirlwind, and I had no time to ask her. Shit. I gotta get to it. We got a candied apple, and as I was gnawing my way through hard sugar I told her about my dream. I said, "It's weird. I have a feeling that you guys have hooked up, and I don't know why." I could just tell by the look on her face that she was guilty. She turned bright red, and it looked like she was gonna cry. My whole body felt hot. I looked over at Athena, and she looked like she had something in her mouth that she couldn't get out. I just yelled at the top of my lungs; I can't remember what I said, but I think it was a guttural "WHHHHY, BITCH???" or "FUCCCCCK YOU, BITCH!!!" and I got up and flipped a chair, which almost hit some stranger sitting nearby. In my peripheral vision I could see people running with their kids 'cause when you're from the Northeast and you see furniture flip, you run. Dee Dee ran the fuck away so fast. Athena came over to try to hold me down, but I flipped her over like a damn pizza. I felt crazy running through this carnival looking for Dee Dee all angry and ugly crying. I must've looked like Jack Nicholson in *The Shining*. Eventually Athena caught up with me and told me I had to go home. I screamed, "Tell me everything you know!" She said it just happened one time. My body felt numb. My heart was in my stomach; I was digesting my actual heart and ready to shit it out. Everything I knew about love and trust and honesty and friendship was out the fucking window. This was the first time I had been in love. I was ready to convert to Islam for this boy. I was saving myself for marriage, and he fucks my best friend. Hakeem called me when I got home. This was before cell phones, and I didn't have a phone in my bedroom, so I had to have this massive breakup call with my dad in the kitchen making dinner. Hakeem was pleading, "I'm so sorry . . . I didn't do anything . . . Can't you forgive me? . . . Let's talk about this."

He was all over the place. He didn't do anything, what do I know? I know it's not true.

I could hear the panic in his voice. "What do you need me to do? I'll do anything for you."

I said, "You'll do anything for me? What about keeping your dick in your fucking pants and not fuck my best friend, you asshole!" I hung up, and my dad was seasoning a chicken breast trying not to say anything. I knew he wanted to though.

"What, Dad . . . ?"

Still seasoning the chicken: "Keep his dick in his pants? Wow. You are my daughter."

Your first breakup is next-level depressing. The sad songs, the not eating, the crying into a pillow all night. I remember Jodeci's remix of Stevie Wonder's "Lately" was playing on the radio and I was all, "Dis for me! Because lately I have been staring in the mirror!"

I didn't talk to Hakeem or Dee Dee after that. My heart was broken. I couldn't trust anyone for a long-ass time. Not boys, not friends. That was my introduction to love, and it fucked me up for a good while. All throughout my twenties, if I had a friend around someone I liked, I was like a watchdog. I had to see if there were any looks between them I was missing. Did he watch her leave the room? Was she looking at him too long? I was a mess. I couldn't confide to my girlfriends fully about someone I liked because I thought they would use that against me and tell the boy. I didn't know if I was worthy of love. Years later, being on the other side of the mountain, I'm really glad I got to experience that shit in my teens. I have friends going through infidelity later in life and they're a mess. I get it. You don't know it at the time, but this rough shit just makes you stronger than you could ever be.

About twenty years later I got a message via Facebook from Hakeem. It was a long, considerate, apologetic email. I was already booed up and married; it had been so long that I didn't even think it was him. I thought it was high school spam. He said that he had a hard time since we broke up and he was ashamed of how we left things because he did in fact love me. He said that I was the one that got away. He said that he believes in karma and that his life hasn't been the same since. His wife up and left him and their kids to fend for themselves. And could I find it in my heart to forgive him so he could move on to the next phase of his life? I made sure the "Read" button was on and never replied. Around that time I was on *Last Comic Standing*. Dee Dee saw me and reached out again, via Facebook as well, and said, "You look so great! You're so funny! How ya been?" I replied, "Still trying to trust people, bitch."

Fuck the both of them.

UNLIKELY ROM-COM

The nineties, for me, was a time that was full of newness and the excitement that comes with that. I had just moved to Miami to go to college, and my whole family followed suit. 'Cause God forbid my Jamaican CSI mother let me go anywhere where she wasn't in arm's reach of my diary and my life! The minute I got accepted to a school in Miami, my mother started making money moves like Cardi B. Her quickness was biblical, "Where you go, I follow" type shit. Except shouldn't there be an invitation? But I didn't care. Everything was full of possibility. Girls were wearing their overalls with one strap down. I didn't because my titties need two straps and a bungee cord system, but still there was something hopeful about it. I mean, Arsenio Hall was riling up the Dog Pound, the Fresh Prince picked a fight and moved to Bel-Air, Biggie Smalls was alive, Diddy was Puff Daddy (which is much more "magical" sounding), and I wanted nothing more than to be a Fly Girl on *In Living Color*. And here I was starting a whole new chapter. I was a

29

freshman in college, and when I wasn't in class, I was at the Reggae clubs dancing in some cargo pants with some fresh black lipstick and some handcuffed-size hoop earrings, just in case the right man wanted to get arrested.

The smoke machine was on full tilt, and Lady Saw and Beenie Man's "Healing" had the floor bumping and thumping. The smoke cleared, and there he was . . . this gorgeous, chiseled dude with his gold chains and khakis. All I could think was, How *do I talk to him?* How *do I get to him?* So I inched my way over to him, and we started doing that dancing thing where you roll your bodies into each other and every time I rolled toward him I got a nice whiff of that Drakkar Noir. He made me feel just right, in all the wrong places! I'm telling you, my heart was beating right out of my chest. In an instant, I felt like a Puerto Rican Molly Ringwald.

His name was "Rojo," he told me. We danced ourselves into a nice sheen, and when the night was over he walked me to my car. That's when I realized we had the same car because he started screaming, "We got the same car!" We both had the same car leased by our moms, but we got to drive them. And I thought, *That's it. We were meant to be.*

"What are the chances? Out of all the dance clubs, you walked into this one; out of all the leasable cars, our moms leased the same model?" He was eighteen, too, and worked but also sold weed and all I could think was, *That means he runs his own business, and he counts fast. These are good qualities!* He also made me feel good about me. You know there's a famous quote, "People will forget what you said, people will forget what you did, but people will never forget how you made them feel"? Well, Rojo made me feel *good*. He was a real accepting person. He made me feel good about my body and confident when it came to sex. I had never felt that before. So, no question, I was in love.

Love leads to plans, and I had big plans. We were going to get married and have kids and get a nice condo with beige carpet and white blinds controlled by a homeowner's association, right in the heart of the suburbs. Once a week we were going to go to the movies, and then maybe even Olive Garden or the Cheesecake Factory. Basically, I was thinking he was my "American dream," and we were going to live it. We started going on vacations together. Our families became entwined. He was everything. It was everything. Until it wasn't.

One night I had this dream. It was all about Rojo telling me he hadn't graduated high school. I thought it was ridiculous. I called him up to tell him about it because I thought it was really funny. I reach the part where he hasn't graduated high school and suddenly there's this deafening silence on the other end of the line. Rojo broke down. Turns out, he had *not* graduated high school. That wasn't all. "I also can't read," he said. *What? What?! Whaaaatttt?!* Now I was seeing some other signs. There was the weird fact that he had zero pictures of himself as a kid around his house. Even his mom had zero pics of him. We always went to the same restaurant. I'm guessing because he memorized the menu and the menu had

31

pictures of the food on it. I would write him poems, but he would always ask me to read them out loud because he said he liked my voice. But, I kept thinking, *How can he* not *read? Haven't we read something together? A newspaper? The instructions on a pregnancy test?* There had to be something. But, nope. He couldn't read.

Well, I wasn't going to let this little bump in the road derail our forever plans, especially after he told me why he couldn't read. When he was young, his dad died. His mom worked three jobs just to get them through. He was depressed and dropped out of the fifth grade. His mom couldn't deal. All I could think was that it was pretty impressive that a guy could get through the modern world without this. He had to be fairly resourceful, right? So I was on his side. I was going to fix it.

The very next day, I went to the library and I made him a "Time to Get Your Ass to Read" SURVIVAL KIT. It was a full-on game plan. It had a list of places to go for night school, a therapist to contact, adult reading books for people learning to read—it was full of helpful tips and tricks. I gave it to him, and he was overwhelmed by it. But I got it. I mean, I'm dyslexic, and even that can be a lot. So I could understand the terror he had.

At first, it was all good and he was on board. But then, after a while, it became obvious that he hadn't taken any action. He didn't want to. Then I started to realize the literacy problem was *my* problem. He wasn't all that bothered by it. I stopped being the girlfriend and I started becoming his coach and his mom. I tried everything, though, and *none* of it worked. Then I backed off. But it was too late. The no-can-read problem was bleeding into everything. When I was happy, I snapped myself out of it. I would remind myself that there was a big problem and that we had to fix it before everything could be okay. Plus, he wasn't even trying. He was not going to reading class. If he had gone to reading class, it would've been okay, right? If he loved me enough, he would learn to read, right? I couldn't talk to anyone about it because I didn't want to embarrass him. I wanted him to feel like a man, so I just carried it. But it weighed on me. We weren't holding hands. We weren't having sex.

I started to resent his illiterate ass. Then I started to see even more signs that were saying, *He gots to go.* One example: he didn't like dark meat when it came to his chicken, so his arroz con pollo was dry as fuck. And wasn't I the dark meat in this arroz con pollo situation?

RED FUCKIN' FLAG. This bitch was never gonna learn to read. I started to think, *ROJO QUE NO SE PUEDE LEER, ADIOS!* (Loose translation: Rojo, who can't read . . . bitch, bye!) Think about it. How was he going to read our kids to sleep after a night out at Olive Garden and before late-evening amazing sex? He wasn't going to. He was going to hum or make up shitty stories or some other unacceptable shit. I was done.

Sure, he could have John Cusack'd the situation by

doing the illiterate man's version of holding up a boom box outside my window. All he had to do was lie down and read some Shakespeare to me in a slow-jams voice. That would've been a panties-off moment for me. It might've sealed the deal. But he didn't. In hindsight, that's all good. 'Cause I've learned, every relationship is wrong until one is right. And a bitch has got to have at least some motivation and ambition to be with me. That's a *must-have*.

Since those hopeful, big-haired nineties days, I've made peace with my first love. I put Rojo Davis in my act, which is the highest compliment I can pay somebody. Sure, my friends say, "Aren't you worried about putting him in your book? What if he gets mad?" But you know what? Bitch can't read.

YA-YA SISTAH HOOD OF THE TRAVELING TANK TOP

I chose to go to school in Miami because I needed to be around people that looked like me. I needed to hear accents besides Vinny at the Jersey Shore. I'd only been there several times for weekend family trips that consisted of hanging at my uncle and aunt's house, eating jerk chicken and cleaning their kitchen. I mean, when your family is from the Caribbean, it's a no-brainer that you'll have family in either Miami or Brooklyn. I'm pretty sure there's a rumor going around in the islands that the streets are paved with gold. But every time I went to a store in Miami they were always playing Gloria Estefan's "Rhythm Is Gonna Get You," and I'd be like, *When?! When is the rhythm gonna get me?* I ended up going to a Catholic university called St. Thomas in Opa-locka, Florida. Opa-locka in Miami is comparable to Compton in Los Angeles.

There's heart and soul to the city, mixed with gold teeth, cornrows, and guns. Lots of guns. But I had listened to enough gangsta rap and gotten in enough fights to feel like I could hold my own. Bish, please. When I landed in South Florida, it was the midnineties; I had no idea what to expect. The Miami airport was sunny and bright and full of everything flamingo. There were all types of brown people walking around in short shorts, sunburned white people with first-grade Serena Williams braids and lots of DSW primary-colored plastic stripper shoe situations. It was exciting as fuck.

My RA showed me to my room and said, "Wear sunblock 'cause you mad yellow; and dem ain't fireworks at night, it's gunshots; I'm finna go to the sto', need somethin'?" Um, yeah . . . sunblock? When I walked around my campus everything smelled like pineapple or some sort of citrus. Everyone was super tan, and their clothes were tiiiiiight. It didn't matter if they were skinny, tall, curvy, short, pregnant. They were *loud* and *proud*. In Jersey, everyone's thing was trying to look the same, but this wasn't the case in Miami. There were Amazon-looking bishes with Daisy Dukes, a tribe of guys that looked like Dominican baseball players complete with cocoa skin, green eyes, and patent-leather dress shoes with sweat socks. I was in a Different World but I hadn't found my Dwayne Wayne. I loved it.

The first week of school I met three girls on my floor that would change my life. Tina lived across the hall from me. She was very tall, had a short bob haircut, and a big-ass crazy laugh. It was so loud it sounded like she needed an EpiPen. She looked like Goofy and Halle Berry had a baby. Even though she was a freshman she was three years older than me. Tina had dropped out of school for a little bit because she had three kids. She'd wanted to get her life back on track then return to school to support her family. She was the most independent woman I'd ever met. Even though she looked like a man from the back and had an Adam's apple for days, guys could not get enough of her. People loved to talk to her when we were in line anywhere. Asian people would ask to take a picture with her 'cause they legit thought she was some kind of mythological creature or something. Everyone assumed she played basketball or was a model because she was so tall. I could see why she had so many kids. People were just attracted to her larger-than-life spirit. As positive and gregarious as she was, she'd also tell someone where to go and how to get there. She had a way with words; she'd read them like a Julia Sugarbaker monologue from *Designing Women*. Her go-to outfit would be cutoff jean shorts, a V-neck white T-shirt, and black gelled curlicues on her forehead. Like a gangsta Josephine Baker.

Then there was Ciara, who lived next door to me. She was a Miami native and started school four months pregnant. Ciara had a sturdy gait and was very curvy—she kind of looked like a young Madea, with all the hips and confidence for days. I couldn't tell she was pregnant because she never wore maternity clothing. She said it was a waste of money and a scam. Plus she explained to me that the women in her family carry their pregnancies in their asses and their noses. I thought Ciara was the smartest person I'd ever met.

Even though she was from the hood, she would speak in these run-on sentences like Olivia Pope in *Scandal*. She never, not once, bought a book to study from; she'd just end up borrowing books from cute boys she happened to have sex with. Apparently you're very horny when you're pregnant, and when momma's happy, baby's happy. I vividly remember seeing young guys doing the walk of shame from Ciara's dorm room shirtless because she'd talk them into giving her their shirts! She never bought anything, ever. Toward the end of her pregnancy, she'd just sport her jeans unbuttoned with a shirt that barely fit over it. It was a mess, but a proud mess. If anyone said anything to her sideways she'd make them feel two inches tall for shaming a pregnant woman. It was amazing to watch. Ciara was *truly* my first encounter with Black Girl Magic.

Then there was my roommate Amelia. She was this tiny, petite nugget from Kingston, Jamaica, who had never left the island. She was very prim and proper. I had never met anyone like her before, very book smart but had no common sense. She didn't know how to make her bed, fold clothes, or even use a washer and dryer because she always had a maid doing these things for her in Jamaica. Amelia was also really into matching. Like if she had a yellow shirt on, there had to be yellow pants, yellow shoes, and yellow jewelry. She was like a light-skinned Elle from *Legally Blonde*. Amelia was like the little sister I never wanted. I had to teach her how to insert a tampon, and I can never unsee that.

Freshman year was uh-mazing. We all couldn't be more different, but we were thick as thieves. It was so refreshing to hang with girls that were from different walks of life. We all had our separate styles, we kinda looked as if the casts from *Girlfriends* and *Sex and the City* had a baby and then that baby went to Maury Povich to find out who the daddy was. These girls helped me break out of my wannabe gangsta-bitch moment and make the jump to my hoochie-momma phase. I traded in my baggy pants for a short denim skirt! Who did I think I was? Da Brat on *TRL*? We would hit up under-twenty-one clubs like we were 702 about to perform. Even though we all had different body types we would share our clubbing clothes as if it was our weekend uniform. Our staples included two black polyester halter tops, a white miniskirt that we had all gotten our period in at some time, yellow pants that looked like culottes on Tina . . . and a black minidress that Ciara had no doubt stretched out. We were the Ya-Ya Sistah Hood of the Traveling Tank Tops.

One night we went to a very popular club on South Beach. It's called Cameo, and it was college night. Because it was an open bar with peach schnapps before midnight, they'd call it Cami-hos. We got there at 10:00 p.m. and I drank all the schnapps. By 11:00 p.m. I was wasted and falling down. By 11:30 p.m. the lights were out in my head, it was very dark, and I don't remember a damn thing. I woke up the next morning in my bed with one of Tina's white V-neck tees with stains all over it. Apparently I got so drunk that these girls had to escort me out, and Tina, of course, slung me over her shoulder like a first responder. No taxi wanted to take me because I was a hot mess, but Ciara talked one guy into taking me. Okay, she threatened to report him to the taxi company for leaving a girl intoxicated. None of us had any money, so Amelia ended up using her rich Jamaican dad's credit card, since this was deemed an emergency. Tina undressed me like I was one of her kids and made sure I had a bucket next to my bed. Of course I felt like soft-serve shit in the morning, but I also felt so lucky to have these bitches in my corner.

The most important thing I learned freshman year in college was acceptance. Who knows if we would have ever been friends unless we lived on the same floor? We all had such different backgrounds, bodies, and goals in life. But what matters is that we had each other's backs. I had never felt that before. I talked about it a ton but never felt it. It didn't matter what these girls were facing in their lives, they were proud of themselves and open to learning new things about different people. They taught me how to walk straight, don't start shit but don't take shit, don't apologize to anyone for anything, and there's nothing wrong with not knowing everything. My most noteworthy teachable life moments I learned in a borrowed tank top.

FRIENDSHIP

As an only child, I was so desperate for siblings. I literally told my father if he ever had a love child, I'd be more than cool with it. I actually suggested some nice ladies I knew from church. I've always wanted a brother or sister, and I mean it! People assume only-children are just out here sitting on a throne opening presents, having rose petals tossed at their feet while someone else is brushing their teeth, but this ain't Zamunda, bitch. You learn to have a good imagination because you're always playing by yourself, and it really affects you. The biggest issue is that later in life you have no one to talk shit about your parents to. I know, I'm probably romanticizing sibling relationships 'cause the grass is always greener when you're standing in shit. But from what I've seen, sibling love looks cute as fuck. You guys are always each other's maid of honor and best man and, eventually, godparents to your kids. You don't have to think about who your best friend is in life because you already had a starter kit at home. I know there are only-children who love being alone, but I'm not that person. I like company. Good company, bad company, crazy company, company that ends up in prison. I don't give a fuck, I can't stand being alone. I leave the TV on when I'm home alone, and I even talk to it sometimes.

I'm only in my forties (damn I look good, though, don't I?) and can't pretend that I know how all of life goes. But I will say this: I've had a lot of friends. Different kinds of friends, from all walks of life. When you're a kid who moves around a lot from an early age, goes to different schools, in different states, following your dad on business trips to different countries, you get real good at introducing yourself. My husband calls me a friend hoarder. He's not wrong, but I love my motley crew of friends. Here's a little guide to help you through the different types of friends you might have at one point.

THE WORK WIFE

This is that coworker you go hard for. The one you immediately are drawn to because they're not an asshole and don't take life too seriously. I've met some of the coolest people at work.

Back when I was editing the local news I met this girl named Hannah whose claim to fame was being a Black girl named Hannah. I'd learn later on that's the only thing she had going on for her, if I had to be honest. She was really charming at first. We'd laugh all the time about the dumbest shit. We'd feel like little brown-titty unicorns because we were definitely the "diversity hires," which is saying a lot because in Miami everyone is a minority! While we'd edit footage of house fires and other mundane shit for the news we'd also sneak in a joint or a plastic cup of wine here and there and fantasize about what we wanted to do in life. I wanted to be an entertainment reporter, and she wanted to be a famous musician and actress. We were gonna take over the world! Okay let's be real—our local five-mile radius.

We were going to move to New York the same year and work at the same job being the diversity hires for some other local station, of course! And we did that! We painted New York City red, fuchsia, scarlet, all the damn colors. We had a ball. We'd get a free appetizer at the Chinese restaurant 'cause we were so cute and happy. We'd get a buyback at the local watering hole near work 'cause we were amazing! When we'd go out people often thought we were related, but we looked nothing alike. We were also the only two Black girls at work, so people always confused our names. People always assumed that she was the older sister, which made her mad (even though she was older). There were also a few times that people thought she was my young mom. OHHHHHHHH she did not like that one bit. She'd always get mad at me as if it were my fault. I realized that was her thing: getting mad. We'd go to bars and pubs, and guys she liked would hit on me and she'd always get mad at me for it.

These guys from Italy moved into Hannah's building, and they were very cute. One of them wanted to go out on a date with me. I didn't know—Hannah told me. I said, "Dope, I'll bring my Rosetta Stone, let's do this." The guy was aight, not really my type, but sweet. He looked like Adrien Brody with curly hair. We went out for Italian, LOL, of course, 'cause he had to prove himself. Went back to his apartment to make out, and he asked me if he could wear my shoes. I said, "Yes, huney, live your journey, but I'm gonna go home when you're done." It was wild! The next day I was so excited to call Hannah and tell her what happened. She didn't pick up. In fact, she ignored me for three weeks. Which was hard, because she was my work wifey. We made a vow that even if we had a moment we would never let it affect our work. We had to have a united front as the only two Black girls at the job. Representation was important and bigger than whatever the fuck nonsense was going on between us.

She eventually asked me out for a drink and confessed that she was mad at me for going out on a date with low-budget Adrien Brody. Even though she had set it up, she liked him as well. I really had no damn idea. If your friend is always mad at you, it's not up to you to guess: *talk* it out! Hannah said she worked up enough courage to ask him on a date. She hooked up with him, and when they were still in bed he asked her if he could wear her underwear and be photographed. I said, "I coulda told you that, bish, but you never picked up the damn phone!"

I don't talk to Hannah anymore. Even though I loved my work wife, we needed to divorce 'cause that shit got messy. After you separate, you have to split your time with the different coworker friends you have in common. You have to pick which days you can show up to the party so you won't see them. Shit gets awkward. It's all good though. The one thing I learned from Hannah is how to look for red flags in friendships. Sometimes people just don't have a bad day. Sometimes they love being miserable.

THE BAD INFLUENCE

This friend is hella confusing because at first you think that they're a free spirit, but nah. They're just fucking up and trying to take you down with them. They're like a Tasmanian Devil of crazy. It's like when someone starts to tickle you and you think it's hilarious, then after ten minutes you're like, *This hurts! Stop! Why are we still doing this?* That friend was Ashanti. She had perfectly brown-lined lips and looked like the poster child for nineties female rappers. I thought she was so cool and fun. Then we went out for Taco Bell after school one day and she offered me cocaine. De fuck? I didn't even know how to respond. For me, Taco Bell has the same effect as cocaine, so why would we have to do cocaine? We were seventeen years old. We're not middle-aged sweaty-ass Cuban pimps! I was a late bloomer, so my go-to in peer pressure situations was always: "No, thanks, it makes me shit so bad."

That was the best, easiest way to get out of weird situations but maintain a sense of cool. Or at least I'd like to think. It's kinda like calling in sick to work because you've got period cramps. Nobody wants details, so they you give you a pass. I wasn't down with drugs, but I was very down with dancing. One night Ashanti convinced me to sneak out of my parents' house to go to a twenty-one-and-under club that had a dance contest. I don't know if I've mentioned that there is a dancer stuck inside my body? She has good knees and zero wedgies in a light purple leotard with dark purple tights #thatprincelife. She's dying to get out, but yeah, she there. My favorite movies were *Dirty Dancing*, *Footloose*, *Fame*, and *Set It Off*. Okay, *Set It Off* isn't necessarily about dancing, but it's about brown-titty empowerment, so gimme a break.

When we got to the club it looked like everyone was a *16 and Pregnant* alum. They were all my age, but these kids looked like they had been through some shit. Which made me look like a PYT. I ended up meeting a Mexican dude named Henry. Which is like, when the fuck would that ever happen? He was so sweet and looked and sounded like the brother in *La Bamba*. The one that couldn't deal with all of Ritchie's success and attention. Even though I just met Henry and I barely knew him, I loved him. I was seventeen and Henry was my destiny. We danced all night in our Karl Kani and Cross Colours, and we won fourth place in the couples' competition. I've never been prouder! My hair was sweaty and jacked-up, and poor Henry tried to help me handle my kitchen. (Kitchen is the lil' naps on the back of a Black woman's neck. Now you know everything.) Before I knew it, it was 4:30 a.m.! I had snuck out at midnight! My parents were about to get up for work! Ashanti tried to convince me to go to Denny's after, but I couldn't. I had to go home; my parents and I shared a car. She tried to guilt me and say, "If you go, I gotta go." Um, so let's go then, bitch? We argued for a bit, but I stood my ground. I was about to agree to stay with her, just because she was so aggressive it was hard to say no. I dropped her off and went home, where I quietly opened the door. I tiptoed ever so carefully up the stairs . . . to find both my parents waiting on the couch for me. I've never felt so bad and guilty and terrible in my whole life. I tried to get out of it by saying, "But I could dance and I felt free . . ." I was praying maybe Patrick Swayze, #restinpower, would come to my defense and take Baby out of her corner. Well, that's the last shit you wanna say to your parents. I was so grounded. For two whole months. That's *two*—too damn long for a seventeen-year-old! It felt like forever, but honestly, I get it now. It's not safe for kids to be out there with Ashanti.

When I went to my room and took my clothes off that night I found a one-hundred dollar bill in my pleated khakis and a note from Henry. It read, "Loved having that chance to dance and romance. Here's some money I put in your pants to fix your hair. Con amor, Henry xoxo." Henry, if you're out there and reading this: You is smart. You is kind. You is important.

By the way, the bad-influence friend doesn't necessarily have to be the good-time party person. They can also love misery. Keep your eyes peeled for the friend who loves to eat terrible-ass beige fried shit all the time and shames you for not taking part in it every Friday night. Look, I don't mind a chicken wing and mozzarella stick once in a while, but I can't just be walking around with coupons to Applebee's. These bad influencers are living life like it's a holiday episode on the Food Network. And they try to shame you for not taking a shot with them. I just tell them, "Stop trying to control me, Dirty John!" You can use that if you'd like. Ashanti was very charming. If I didn't have strict immigrant parents constantly on my dick about going to college and not getting knocked up, who knows? I might have happily and nappily gone along with her shenanigans like an episode of *Orange Is the New Black*, complete with backstory.

THE TRAVEL BUDDY

Are you cheap? Do you like to stay in hostels? Do you get a boner eating at some hole-in-the wall place like you're Anthony Bourdain? Well, I don't wanna play the cards like that. This is why the right travel buddy friend is 100 percent necessary, especially when you are in your midtwenties. Okay, for the rest of your life! People travel in different ways. Some friends love making plans with a map like a big-tittied Christopher Columbus; going to every museum, finding your way to the world's largest ball of yarn, some creepy graveyard, or whatever. No, thank you. Not unless we've got bikes and some edibles. I mean, I don't mind a light hike, but I'm also gonna need a cute IG pic at a good restaurant. I found my travel partner in crime in college. Cynthia and I were in the same TV production class, and we were nothing like the other students. They were so intense they would dress like Rachel Maddow and quote Spielberg when they weren't even in class. Reelax! Meanwhile Cynthia and I closely studied footage from MTV's *Spring Break* and saved up our pennies in college to go to Cancun. We did all the free activities involved with the hotel: parasailing, ATV rides, a weird morning snorkel session on a boat where I got to look at coral while hungover. Cynthia definitely threw up a little bit over the side of the boat. Which was nice because it attracted more clownfish. And that's when you know you have the perfect travel buddy.

For the next ten years through our twenties we ended up traveling everywhere. We were like a low-budget *Eat Pray Love*. We would cash in our tax returns and make it happen. We went to Paris on Air India and made out with French dudes. We motorboated bread and had purple-stained lips from all the red wine in Mont-Saint-Michel. We visited Argentina, where we went to see Lenny Kravitz and we got interviewed by MTV Latino afterward for being cool-looking and also not white. I forgot my ATM card in a machine in Buenos Aires because I was so high that, after it sucked my card in, I forgot it would give it back after my withdrawal. Confusing!

We went to Spain, got tapas, and then got topless on

the beach. We rented bikes (not topless) and lost each other for the day, then found each other by accident. We went to Ireland and met everyone who lives in Dublin in one day. Then we river-danced to live fiddle music in a pub like two young curly-haired Taylor Swifts at the Grammys.

For my thirtieth birthday we went to South Africa and Botswana. That shit was so damn magical, I wrote a one-person show about it and Cynthia was the technical director. It was called *Thirty Years in Africa*, and no one came to see it. In hindsight, that's a terrible-ass name. But we had a bomb-ass time. In Cape Town we visited townships and hugged children who all thought I was fat Beyoncé. It was truly amazing. We went dancing, and I invited people I drunkenly met that night to stay at my place in New York when they came to America. I'm so happy that no one took me up on it. We went on a safari in Botswana and saw the "big five," which is not an episode of *Keeping Up with the Kardashians*. The travel buddy is a special friend, 'cause you can go anywhere with them, and it's always fun. They're basically a nomadic roommate who understands what needs to happen and not happen in your life.

THE SPONGE

Oh. This. Bitch. The sponge friend is a fun one. You feel free as fuck, as if you could say anything to them. These friends say "Yes, and" like they're in improv class, and you think you're twinning in a safe space. Then you slowly but surely realize that they're just regurgitating stuff from other people, including you. You don't know it till they've hung with you for so long they start saying shit you say, as if they've made it up themselves. That's the scariest shit and the closest thing to knowing a sociopath. I don't wanna name names, but stand-up comics have been known to do this. Stealing bits of personality and jokes onstage isn't the same as saying "y'all" after you've been hanging around your friend from Alabama. I've tried to call people out on this behavior, but they completely deny it. It's so frustrating. You work up the nerve to tell someone that they've been stealing your words, phrases, and POV, and they completely shut you down. This has happened to me more than once. One of my friends even got successful from using my personality onstage. It's like a *Freaky Friday* movie with no happy ending. It's hard to recognize these people right away, because they're just so damn charming. But if someone's repeating what you've said in social situations, and in your head you're thinking, *Bitch, you owe me residuals by now!*, don't give them your shine.

THE CRAZY BISH

This could literally mean anything to anyone. The crazy-bish friend runs the gamut. This friend is the wild card you invite to a party because you know they'll spice shit up. You know they have "a good heart," so you try to explain away the dumb shit they do. They've always got a story about how someone or something wronged them. They're always a victim. Either someone hasn't paid them or picked them up or they've gotten hurt or lost and it's always a good-ass story! These people are the life of the party but also the death of the party. There are the ones that get the dance floor going at a wedding but also get in the fight at the dessert buffet 'cause someone's "disrespected" them. I have plenty o' craycray bishes in my life. I think it's because they're my type. Maybe I'm theirs? I just know how to handle the crazy, since my family is very crazy . . . um . . . emotional . . . um . . . Caribbean? One of my white friends at my wedding got so drunk (I mean, everyone did), but she truly lost her mind over three glasses of wine, which is just dinner or a plane ride for me. She tried to freestyle rap at one of my homeboys (who's Black) and was unsuccessful at making it rhyme, which made him feel uncomfortable enough to ask me to be his security during the Soul Train line. She. Was. A. Mess. And I'm sorry, not sorry—I enjoyed the fuck outta it.

Then there's the crazy-bish friend who's such a hot mess it's like, how are they an adult in the world without hurting themselves or getting lost every ten minutes? I've had a friend since high school that I tried to keep in my circle, but it's very hard keeping up with all his messes. I don't have enough brooms. We'll go out and he's charming, everyone loves him, he dresses great, we get a free drink or some shit then— bam!—the bill comes. Reality sets in, and this muthafucka ain't never got no money to pay for his shit. And it's always "Just this one time," so you end up paying for him. Partly because you feel bad but mostly because you don't want to look like an asshole after he got us a round of free drinks. Then we'll go out dancing and drinking and he'll know people at the club for a table and this and that bottle service. Oh shit, the DJ is giving us a shout-out, ain't he cool? Then—bam!— reality sets in: this muthafucka lives deep in the Bronx and can't afford a taxi home. His train is so far away from his new apartment because he had to move out of his penthouse in Tribeca because one of the girlfriends in his throuple relationship went back to her other wife because she gave her the money she needed for her start-up scarf-making company for Etsy and he can give me a discount but can he sleep on my couch? What the fuck and so on and so forth. It's exhausting. I need electrolytes after I hear about his drama.

The good thing about being married to an honest European person with a handful of friends is that he does not suffer fools. Husband liked my friend Travis, but one of the times he had to sleep over after being out all night with us, Travis drunkenly went into our fridge and ate every piece of a week's worth of Italian deli meat we had just bought that day. I don't eat prosciutto, but I got it for Husband because it's his favorite. This muthafucka went through a half pound of prosciutto by himself. Do you know how much work it is to unwrap each piece like a tiny, pricey Christmas present and just go for it? He's treating Genoa salami like potato chips!

I'd had enough. I told him he needed to get out and I couldn't do this anymore. See, it's hard to put the crazy-bish friend in their place. It's just who they are; they can't help it. But you can! They're fun in big settings, but one-on-one you're always doing damage control. Recognize this shit before this friend is inappropriate with everyone in your friends-and-family plan and eats you out of house and home. Who knew that cured meats would be the straw that breaks the camel toe?

THE PERFECT-ON-PAPER BUT MIND-NUMBINGLY-BORING FRIEND

This friend does all the things one should do when they come over. They arrive on time. They always ask beforehand what they should bring and they brang it. They wait in that forty-five-minute line at the hottest bakery to get the overpriced cronut. These people you wanna be friends with, yes. They're honest and sweet and pure and just so nice. They might have a kill room or a weird porn collection, 'cause you don't know people's lives. They always do the right thing. But they truly have no fucking personality at all. You have to constantly think of a conversation starter. I try to find places for them all the time. Invite them to a big dinner party at my house so I don't have to do a one-on-one with them. But oh man, they always get lost in the sauce like the new shy kid at school. These friends always help to clean up too. They're like the nice person you keep dating just because you feel like you need to be reminded that people can be nice. I'm not saying this to be a bitch, but I don't want to feel like I need to entertain everybody all the damn time. That's how the perfect-on-paper but mind-numbingly-boring friend makes you feel—like you have to take care of them. That's probably why they're attracted to you as a friend as well, because they don't have to do much. They've got social anxiety, and you're the fun, safe place.

It's exhausting being friends with people like this. You get a glimmer of happiness and hope, then it goes back to silently cleaning countertops of artisanal crumbs. Plus a ton of guilt. You'll need a quiet friend, though. Not a gang of them, but definitely a smattering. They think before they act and if you're like me, you need someone like that to bounce off of. Speak up, honey, if you're the quiet person! You don't have to give a town hall speech at the dinner party, but your voice is worthy!

THE BAD DATE THAT TURNED OUT TO BE A GOOD FRIEND . . . 'CAUSE WHO KNEW?

It's the opposite of every rom-com: What if in *When Harry Met Sally* they went out on a date, it was lukewarm, and then they decided to be good friends for a minute, and that was it? Yeah, boring, but real as fuck. I went on a date one time using a website called BlindDate.com and yep, you guessed it, I wouldn't know who I was dating till I met them in person!

What a genius website title. When you log on, you enter your information, answer some random questions about turn-ons and turn-offs, ya know the regular run-of-the-mill shit, then you upload a picture. But the catch is—when people see your profile, it's pixelated.

I was set up with someone immediately. I didn't know much about him except that he was a tall, attractive Black dude. When I tried to look at his picture, it was so pixelated he just looked like Janet Jackson's nipple at the Super Bowl. (May that areola moment rest in power.) I met homeboy at a cool, laid-back, Afropunk-chic place. I didn't know who I was looking for, but I spotted the tallest, biggest brotha in the vicinity and knew immediately that it was him. He was sweet, and warm, and he kinda talked like the dude from *The Green Mile*. We tried to find seats at the lounge, but we couldn't find one to fit his body. He was a huge nerd. He looked like Shaquille O'Neal and Urkel had a baby. We finally found a restaurant that fit his big build. It was a pub that just had benches. I really felt for him because he didn't seem like he had fit in many places and therefore was forced to dance to the beat of his own drum.

We were getting to know each other; you know, the first twenty minutes of a date that's just an interview to make sure you're not creepy or annoying. He told me that he likes to go against the grain. Um, okay Forrest Gump, where are we going with this? He said that he "loves Goth." Um, okay, cool. I tried to get along and said, "Well, I had a cousin that was Goth and she loved black-and-white eye contacts and Marilyn Manson." He said that it was so much more to being Goth then that. *Cool, cool. Tell me all about it; I'm here for it.* I like a good Blackstory. He said that he's hard-core Goth (I didn't care) and that if I was in the community that he would know me. (Still don't care.) He told me that he's been Goth for a few years and now he deejays Goth cruises. Wow, that just got worse! How was that possible? It also made me realize that there really is a cruise for everything. I was interested and horrified at the same time. Much like watching a *My Strange Addiction* episode where a woman drinks gasoline every day. You feel weird learning about her, but you just have to know.

What I learned is, apparently, that there is a generation of Goth people who "just wanna go on vacation and take their kids." I started mentally storyboarding Tim Burton's *Gilligan's Island*. Also, I don't know what was more sad: that we had to hit up four Midtown restaurants to find homeboy a chair for his big, Black, Goth booty, or that kids of Goth parents were forced to go on a cruise to the western Caribbean while wearing all black.

We ended the date in a cordial manner. I paid for my own loaded potato skins and Guinnesses 'cause that meant I wouldn't have to touch his Goth dick. It probably had a white contact lens on the end of it. When I got home he had sent me a DM on Myspace. I knew I had to respond immediately because there was the whole "Read" function, which had ended many friendships. He sent me a picture of him in full-on drag looking like the Black Terminator in lingerie. He had on a robot red eye and the other eye was solid black. Full-on Halloween-tired sassy robot makeup; a red corset. I'm not pretending to know all the things about Goth. But I'm pretty sure it didn't involve a red corset for the Shaq O'Neal of Urkels. But also, it should? Don't get me wrong, I'm not judging his journey. I'm just surprised as fuck. By the way, if they haven't already, the site should change its name to Blindsided.com. I wasn't attracted to Urkel O'Neal, but I thought he was honest and wacky. I ended up being peripheral friends with him.

We didn't hang tough, but I would occasionally invite him to a show. I'd make sure he had a chair to fit that massive NBA-size Goth booty and always pointed out from stage that we went out on a date together. We stayed in internet touch. He was a fun New York hang when I was single. Who knew that would be spawned out of a New York City internet blind date?

THE "ACCIDENTAL" RACIST

We all have a friend that's like a goodwilled Archie Bunker. No? Just me? These friends are super cool, then—bam!—out of nowhere they'll say something racist as if it were a burp they had to get out. They even might just like saying racially inappropriate stuff to get a rise out of you. What a waste of my time. My favorite is when people say racist shit when they're drunk and blame it on the drank. Come on, now. Too many tequilas and you're calling the taxi driver a sand nigga? No, mame. No, thank you. I've been blackout drunk (a lot) and you know what I do? Make pancakes and fall asleep on the toilet.

That racist bone is deep-seated. One day I was shopping in Chinatown, NYC, with a coworker I had gotten close to. She was a smart white girl from upstate New York who dated the damn rainbow. She would go to marches and protests and seemed pretty woke. A dress she wanted to buy was on the sale rack, but the Chinese lady cashier explained to us in her broken English that it wasn't on sale. My friend pushed back that it was on the sale rack and she should get the price. They went back and forth for a minute, then my friend yelled, "Just give me the fucking sales price, you chink!" WHAT. THE. FUCK. I was so embarrassed. My whole body turned hot, and I said "I'll pay full price! No worries, thank you!" When we got outside I had to have a come-to-Jesus and break down why that wasn't acceptable. But how did she not know? These words are toxic and you sound ignorant. We are the company we keep. Unless you're ready to be Iyanla Vanzant and hand out teachable moments, don't have the racist friend in your life—no matter how long or well you've known them.

YOU COULDA BEEN A CONTENDAH!

These friends have all the makings of becoming a good-ass bestie, but something happens in the beginning of the friendship that puts a kibosh on that right away. When Husband and I lived in Los Angeles, Husband met a cool dude named Bryan. His wife, Meena, was equally charming. They looked like a boho Pinterest, and I was into all the avocado toast they were serving. Husband and I had also just low-key adopted a dog from a neighbor—I used to walk this little nugget, and her previous owner was pretty much living her life like an episode of *90 Day Fiancé*. When she married her tour guide in West Africa, she was always out of town.

Bryan and Meena invited us over to their apartment for a delicious dinner. In true LA fashion they told us we could bring our dog, because they have a dog and they'd get along. I trusted them. When we showed up their dog wasn't very well behaved or trained. It was sort of nipping "because it was excited" and tailgated Roxy (our dog) everywhere in the apartment. They assured us everything was fine, but I was feeling a little anxious as a new dog owner.

While we were eating the first course of our dinner (seasonal butternut squash soup in a bread bowl), Disco (their dog) wanted to get into Roxy's business. Roxy was by our feet and not into it. She's a small dog and snapped no. Disco didn't like that shit one bit. She took ahold of Roxy by her neck and wouldn't let go. It was the worst noise you'd ever wanna hear. Like a true-life horror movie. Dog fights are the worst. The sounds, the sounds. Have you ever heard kids screaming during dismissal at school? You don't know if they're having an amazing time or killing one another. This was that, minus the possibility that it was an amazing time. I don't know how the dogs did this, but Disco ended up lifting the dinner table and pushing it on its side. All the dinner plates came crashing down. My little dog was in this big dog's mouth like a scene from *Jaws*. I tried to hold Disco down while Husband put his hands in her mouth to get Roxy out. Meena was just screaming in a corner, and Bryan had the quick mind to stick his fingers up Disco's booty so she could release her jaw. And that's what she did. We saw what was left of Roxy. It was an experience I don't wish on my enemy. Her head looked like it was going to fall off. There was blood all over her fur, and skin was everywhere. Husband screamed "Roxy!!" in a way that I've never heard his voice sound.

We ran out to our car and drove to the nearest animal hospital shoeless. Roxy ended up surviving through surgery. Thankfully she had a couple of extra pounds, so there was some skin for the vet to play with. We were crestfallen, though. This was our first dinner party at their house and it turned into a horror movie. When we talked to Bryan and Meena they were pretty upset and very apologetic. They offered to pay half the surgery cost, which was nice of them. They'd call to check in and see how we were doing, which was thoughtful. During one of our recap sessions they expressed that they didn't think this was completely Disco's fault, and that Roxy started it with an attitude. Look, I'm a new dog owner and I'm not the Dog Whisperer, but I do know that if my dog attacked another dog I wouldn't bring up that I think it's not my fault. Yeah, that was the nail in the coffin for me. See you at the funeral because our friendship is #dead.

When my husband and I were in Brooklyn we'd hang tough with a couple we met through friends. They lived in Virginia, used to live in New York, and were always in town. They were so great, just smart, warm, funny, and kind people. So when they offered to house- and dog-sit for us when we went to Holland for family vacation, it was a no-brainer.

Husband had just installed a Nest Cam in the house, which is a camera hooked up to your phone that shows you who's coming in and out of the house. We got one because we kept getting packages stolen by an old-ass, low-budget Flavor Flav–looking muthafucka in the hood. When we woke up to over 150 door open and close notifications in Holland one morning, we had to check the video. There were people coming in and out of the house. Bringing wine, beer, hard liquor, plates, and trays of food. One person had ice. ICE, HUNEY. You know its turn-up time when someone brings ice! The sinking feeling Husband and I had in the pit of our stomachs, I can't describe. It was sheer and utter disappointment. And rage. There were people we didn't know just walking up into our house being greeted by Anthony and Liza. People with dogs and kids. I don't know these dogs. What if something happened with our dog? I know now that's already a thing. What if someone's kid hurt themselves in our home and we're not there? I was so disappointed. We had to make a phone call to them and ask them why they threw a party in our house with over fifty people and not even check in with us? They were very apologetic and said they misread the situation. But the only situation was that they took advantage of us and we didn't see it coming. It sucks because they're such good people. But good people can do bad things sometimes. So do you stick around? I guess if you want to. But I don't. There are plenty of people to hang with that won't take advantage of your generosity and space. We see them from time to time, as we have friends in common, but it'll never be the same. They could've been a contendah!!! But they fucked that up. Fool me once . . . shame on you, bitch. I'm too old for this shit. Now sashay away.

CHOSEN FAMILY

You know who these people are. They're the friends who have your back no matter what. They pick you up when you fall; they talk you off the ledge, they push you to reach for the end of the limb where the sweetest fruit is. (LOL come *on*, I've been reading too many magnets!) When you need to talk something out, you run your shit by them and they're your therapist. And you're theirs. You don't have to know this person long, but you know them well. Really well. This friend isn't afraid to tell you when you're fucking up, and they always have your back.

You need people like this in your life. You need a solid

person you can talk to besides your family members. This friend is like an in-law but just all the good parts. You get to know each other's families; you make memories together. You guys are the reason why Friendsgiving even exists. The reason why there are friend quotes on magnets. I have been lucky enough to have a good amount of friends in my life, so if one pisses me off I can call another one. Just kidding, that's so ignorant. But also, what a great plan. There are friends I'll call up if I have a problem with career stuff, relationship situations. And there is never any judgment. If you have someone like this in your life, call them or text them right now. Tell them that you appreciate them so, so fucking much, 'cause they're your chosen family.

GAME OF HEAUXS

BAD MOUTH

I distinctly remember when I moved to New York City because it was on Saint Patrick's Day. I booked that date on purpose. Not because it's one of the biggest holidays in the city, but because it's cheap as hell to fly to New York when you have to keep lifting your suitcase over puddles of frozen green vomit. I got a job as a video editor at WNBC and was making more money than most of the men in my family. It was insane. I also didn't realize at the moment, but the WNBC TV production crew I was in was a bit of a boys' club. Everyone was older than me and had stories for days. And these people could drink. I thought, *Holy shit, I fucking made it! My people!*

It had been a couple of months, and I was finding my way around the city. Mostly by hanging tough with my co-workers. One in particular, Chris, was jacking me hard. He was nice, street smart. He was still rough around the edges.

Good at remembering batting averages, bad with dental care. His teeth went in so many directions it reminded me of trying to figure out my major: #pullmyfinger. But he had kind eyes. Plus he was one of the only Black dudes that worked on my floor, so I felt like I had to give him a chance.

Not saying if you're Black and we work together we gotta hook up. But I'm not not saying that either. Just that, in corporate America, if you see a Black person your age it's your duty to be friends with them, maybe have sex with them to see what might happen? We've gotta look out for each other.

It was Cinco de Mayo, and Chris showed me a serious New York City–ass night. We went out for drinks, mudslides or smooth criminals. (Sorry, white people, that means Hennessy and Baileys.) I can't really remember much. But I know we got street Halal Chinese Spanish food and suddenly I became a low-budget Padma Lakshmi? We went barhopping to a few more places. And since he was cute enough to easily be in a Fat Joe video, I took him back to my sublet apartment.

I'm not sure if it's more boss or more sad to bring a one-night stand home to a place that's not even yours. I'm gonna stick with boss. The doorman reminded me of Ice-T in *SVU*, just ready to be a character witness. Chris and I started making out in my sublet bedroom, and it was hot from what I remember. But then I felt a little too hot, and not in a good way. First it was a wave of hot, like when you've just texted

Carol a message about how shitty Carol is. Then my stomach dropped to my knees and came back up in my throat, and then I knew nothing good was going to come out of this mouth.

I started to throw up. I'd never experienced anything like this before. Then again, I had never had Irish cream, Hennessy, Halal Chinese Spanish street meat, and tequila before either. I ran to the bathroom while half screaming/half politely singing "I'll be right back!" and slammed the door.

Now, I didn't hug the toilet like people do in the movies. It skeeved a bitch out to put my face in a sublet toilet seat, so I did what I thought was best in the moment and threw up in the tub. That seemed fine. Until I turned the shower on and watched as chunks of sweet-and-sour chicken, yellow-rice-and-bean shawarma platter clogged the fucking drain.

I tried to fish it out with my hands and put it in the toilet while whispering, "Ewww whyyyyyyy yuck ewwwww whyyyyyyyy yuck"—but nothing was working. My tank top was ruined. My spinning head was full of *I hope he didn't see. Did he see? I don't think he saw. NO . . . HE DIDN'T SEE.* I washed my face, brushed my teeth, closed the shower curtain, and sprayed enough Lysol to disinfect a New York City subway. Then as I grabbed the doorknob, I said a little prayer to myself: *Please* don't *let him see, Please* don't *let him see.* And after I convinced myself *I'm good, I'm totally good! He didn't see a damn thing!*, I finally got the nerve to open the door. And then I saw a five-foot-long trail of evidence leading right to the bathroom door. I also saw that he was wiping his arm off with a paper towel. I was mortified.

I walked in and was all "Oh Jesus, are you okay?"

"Yeah, I'm okay. Do you feel better?"

"One hundred percent better."

"Okay, cool."

Then he threw my ass on the bed, ripped my vomit-soaked tank top off, handled me like one of those scenes in a rom-com you've been waiting for. Holy shit it was next level.

I guess when your teeth are that jacked you got something to prove? And he did that. The next morning, he served me some new boyfriend vibes and helped me put together some IKEA furniture. I told him he wins all the rose ceremonies but I'm new to New York and I can't be tied down. He understood and told me to remember to drink water in between drinks next time I'm out. A gentleman and a scholar!

PUTTANESCA

Dating in New York was and will always be tough. It's easy to meet people, hard to get to know them. It's like playing the lottery. You may put in, and you may lose, but hey . . . ya never know. It drives me crazy when people have a few bad experiences and decide to take themselves out of the game. Open your mind, your heart, and your legs, and you will absolutely increase the odds. I'm not saying I was good at it. I can't give you the dos and don'ts, 'cause I'm not Steve Harvey.

I'm just a big-titty bitch that's put in work. In high school and college I was so serious about love, I put my trust and eggs all in one basket. I was completely heartbroken both times. This time I was gonna live my life like it's gold-en gold-en gold gold gold en en en.

New York City is pricey as fuck. If you're not living in sin with someone, you need a roommate. So I rented an apartment with a friend of a friend from Miami and we lived on the corner of Fifty-Sixth Street and Ninth Avenue. Blocks were crowded, restaurants were expensive, and the rats were plenty. I was a regular at all the places in our two-block radius. Particularly, one Italian place on the corner, Puttanesca, which loosely translates to: "Lots of old-ass white people that eat pasta with olives before they go to Broadway shows." One night I was there with a coworker from WNBC. She was from Jersey and was short, but she had really big feet, which made her a bit bossy. She desperately wanted to get married so she could move out of her parents' house. All of this made her the perfect wingwoman. Our waiter that night was so flirty with me I was waiting for a rose ceremony.

He kept asking me if I was okay; but he knew I was perfect-type shit. I was like, *That's so nice, but do we get any free food?* He basically took care of most of our bill, and I was in. Not in love, in debt. I'm in my midtwenties! New York is pricey and I'm here to take all I can fucking get.

We exchanged numbers and went out. He was from Albania, which, to me, seemed exotic. Also where the fuck is that? I usually assume everyone's Puerto Rican. He was super tall. Just, like, so tall, I think six three or six four? And so damn thin. Like people looked at him and thought *Is he okay?* thin.

He spoke just enough English to have a green card and a job, and who doesn't love ambition? I sure do. I'd rather be with someone who's ambitious and has no money than someone who's lazy and has money. We dated on and off for a few months, because I thought it was sexy that I got to eat for free. The only difficult part was his being so skinny. I'm not trying to shame anyone, it's just that his bones would dig into my flesh when he was on top of me having sex. Like, if I had been just as skinny, we would've made a fire. This chicken piccata ain't worth all that. He also wanted to skip using a condom. I'm like, *Come on, honey,* you ain't gonna like how it feels when you have to start working doubles. I mean, look, I didn't really use homeboy for food, that was just a plus. I really liked him, but he was just so boring. No fun stories; didn't get my pop culture references.

I realized I made him more interesting than he was because I loved company. But when you take free malbec out of the equation, it was really just a party of one. So it might as well be that.

Question: Do you know how hard it is to ghost someone that works on your block?

Answer: Very. I took the long way home a lot of the

time. But the plus side is that I got my steps in. Can't hold a big-titty bitch down!

BIG TITTY, LITTLE GUY

Some of my single-ass aunts will say, "Nothing really matters as long as a man can take care of you." And while I'm the first person to give someone a chance, I've also got my limits.

When I first started doing comedy I decided to take a stand-up class to punch up some of my material. There I met the cutest, shortest, most Jewish nugget of a man I'd ever encountered. His name was Seth. Let me tell you, the way he'd stretch his little-ass neck to look up at me melted my cold, cold heart. He was truly the biggest personality in the tiniest body. He wanted to do right by a bitch. And this little-ass man was doting on me *big*-time. But the chemistry was off between us somehow. Maybe because, even when he was rock-hard, I've had pieces of chicken bigger than that in my mouth. Or that one night we were spooning, okay, actually I was just giving him a piggyback ride lying down AND?!?!? Oh mah gawd, real talk—we lay down and my new H&M earrings got tangled in his back hair. I felt like a terrible person, because he loved to take care of me! He'd play his little guitar with his small soft hands and sing me the Beatles in bed. Or make up songs about me? When he starts rhyming my name? That's some panty-dropping shit.

We looked so opposite I couldn't deal. Even if I was

holding his hand, men would still hit on me. He always looked like he should be holding a balloon with his other hand. One night I was doing my thing, trying to feel him somewhere, and he yelled, "Stop! You're hurting me!" What. In. The. Natural. Fuck? I was only giving him like 65 percent. When you find yourself making a pro-and-con list about why you should be together, it's time to go. Especially if the con side just has: "I can't do this shit anymore." If I ever pitch a show to HBO it'll be called *Big Titties, Little Guys*.

DON'T BE A SHERO

If you're ever in New York City it is your duty to go dancing somewhere Spanish and be spun like a dreidel on Hanukkah. I used to frequent this place named Gonzalez y Gonzalez. I met a Dominican dude that was so hot that I totally get why Chantal applied for that K-1 visa on *90 Day Fiancé*. He was fun and sexy and had pro-player baseballer energy. Shit, he even had a pouch of Big League Chew on him. Then, as he popped a huge handful of that amazing shredded bubble-gum into his mouth, he told me, "I liiiike to haaa deee fresh brefff . . ." Okay, his English wasn't deee best, but he wanted to suck my toes, so how could I not? We hopped in a taxi and I thought it'd be a great idea to go down on him in the back seat. A gross yellow-cab back seat that only gets wiped down when someone's thrown up.

Now, we all hear about bad decisions people make, like

super-short retro bangs. But I made an extra bad decision. I decided to go to town on a Dominican dick while I still had Big League Chew in my mouth. As I lifted my head up, I saw a long pink string still attached to his junk. He panicked, and I couldn't stop saying, "*¡Lo siento, boo!*" Ever had this happen? Just me? Cool.

I had the taxi driver stop at a bodega so I could pick up some peanut butter and ice. I don't know about a penis, but I know it'll get gum off your couch, so let's see? Oh, whoops, my bad. All hacks don't always work. My takeaway lesson with this sweat-sock-wearing, patent-leather-shoe-having, bachata-dancing Dominican dude is: don't be a shero. If you're super excited to be with someone next-level hot, that's amazing. Congratulations, you did it! But stay in your lane. Especially in public spaces.

THE ONE

I'm not sure how much you know about comedians, but when they're in their twenties they date one another like horny teenagers at sleep-away camp. I wasn't mad at it, but I couldn't get down with it. Who wants to date a coworker, especially one who could write jokes about you? No, thank you. I did briefly hang out with one comic for a bit. Just to clarify, "hanging out" means you have feelings for someone and those feelings are not mutual. If someone ever describes your relationship as "hanging out," then they are just never gonna give you what you need, bitch. Now that you know, it's on you! After a few months of hanging out with said comedian . . . Christmas came and a bitch didn't even get a card. New Year's came and went, and not even a text. Valentine's Day happened and not even a wad of Big League Chew. I was fed up that a whole season had passed by. This person knew what I felt like but wasn't giving me the commitment I thought I deserved. I thought he would fall in love with me and how cool I am and want more than just a hangout. That never happened.

Finally, after a long night of doing shows together in Times Square, I worked up enough courage to casually ask, "Hey, are ya dating anyone else?" And he said two little words that I will never forget: "Define dating." My mouth dropped. I just stood there speechless. So I finally said, "You know: dating . . . dating dating, *like* . . . who doesn't know what a date or dating is—datinnnggg." He just looked at me like he knew it was over and he was okay with it. Now, I know some might say I'm dramatic, and I'll take it. I looked at him with tears in my eyes and said, "We could've been the Will and Jada of comedy . . ." and walked away. I could feel him waiting for me to turn around, but I wouldn't give him the satisfaction of the one last look back.

What I learned from this hookup is that, when it comes to relationships, I have to act like I'm in a new restaurant. If I want it, I have to ask for it. Just like a waiter, a man can't read my mind to figure out what I want. And I can't assume they'll do what I want unless I put myself out there. But for fuck's sake—*Brotha, we could've been the Will and Jada of comedy?!?!* That is my "I carried a watermelon?" moment from *Dirty Dancing.* Sorry if you're under thirty and reading this: all my pop culture references are older than you.

DICKMETIZED

One thing that gets us all into trouble is ignoring signs that a person just isn't right for you. I've had so many red flags in my life I could host my own Toyotathon. I actually cared for someone who I met on Yahoo! Personals. The thing that attracted me to him the most was his "About Me" that read, "I had an ALF skateboard growing up." That's all it took to peak my interest, a brother who liked ALF? I fell in love with this man-boy who was low-key homeless. He always had a home to stay in, it was just never his. He didn't have a pot to piss in or a window to throw it out of.

I always ended up paying our way because he "was going through stuff" and "life isn't fair" and he "never had a dad, so he doesn't get dad jokes." That's something he actually said. He was one of those lofty, unrealistic-goals guys who had no clue how to get there. He was going to start his own magazine but didn't have a subway card. He wanted to become a poet full-time but thought working in the service industry was beneath him. My dude, the service industry was built for people who want to be full-time poets! But damn, he was a good kisser, and we didn't have sex, we *made love*, huney. Like we were in a movie. He always gently laid me down into a soft bed (my bed), my sheets wrapped around us postcoital. He'd offer pillow talk (free) and a foot massage (also free). He was basically doing lots of whining without the dining. That was a problem. He also had a lot of girlfriends. A lot. Beaucoup. And most of these bitches looked like a version of me. You never really think someone is going to be that fucking obvious, but if you're in a relationship and it stinks like fish, it's probably extra pussy.

I found out that he had been hooking up with one of his friends. We were all out drunk one night and she told me that they had been having sex. She felt bad because she could tell I liked him and that I was being honest. Yeah, I'm being honest. Who the fuck is out here just not being honest? Why is everyone a monster? I broke things off with him. Breaking up with someone that you like but has done you wrong is like getting along with an employee but having to fire them anyway.

Four years later I got a random email list from someone I've never heard of. I opened it to unsubscribe from the list. It was the ALF skateboard guy. He had moved to the Czech Republic and become a successful rapper. I almost didn't recognize the pictures of him because he was wearing clothes other than his navy Champion sweatshirt and oversize brown corduroy jacket. Good for him. Also, FUCK HIM.

Look, some people aren't proud of their past when it comes to bad dates, terrible partners, et cetera. I get it, it's embarrassing. But I decided to take the shame out of my most awkward situations/times in my life and embrace the fuck out of them. It has taken me a good while to stand in power and truth about my past. Too many times women are meant to feel disgraced for owning their sexuality. But if we take back the night, then no one can hold anything over us. I guess what I'm saying is . . . in all my womanly wisdom and after absorbing years of experience in love and lust, I don't stigmatize getting dickmetized. Get it in, get it out, and know how to plan around and manage that shit when you see it happening.

9/11 CHRONICLES

My coworker Beth and I had to work the late shift, midnight to 9:30 a.m., and we were out dipping it and doing it right before. Yes, I had to work; and yes, I kept it professional. I was in my twenties! I wasn't tipsy; I was creative! We were at a pub where two English guys picked us up. I was really impressed by how confident they were for no reason. Despite the stereotype, their teeth were a lot less jacked than Chris's. They were "on holiday" to New York for the first time, and they were loving life. I was into that. The English bloke (I know things) that liked me was named Noah. He kept buying rounds, asking questions about America, had his arm around my chair—ya know, giving me all the signs that he was really into me. I felt like he was my prince and I was his Cinderella because I had a midnight call time!

It was September 10, 2001, and I worked my usual shift. I also shared my usual peanut M&M's with my writer Stephen. It was a regular-ass new day and we thought we were gonna sneak out a little early, at our usual time around 9:15 a.m. But at 8:46 a.m. the worst possible thing ever happened. An object, we weren't sure what, flew into the World Trade Center. We didn't know what happened or why, but the only thing we were told to do is roll on it. Keep recording it. If anything happened at a certain time, write it down for reference. In the news business, drama isn't good enough until it's followed by more drama. At this point we just thought it was breaking news. The way we'd roll on a house fire or any other accident. We had live coverage with anchors talking over live video about what they think could have happened and what people must be going through.

Then we saw another object fly into the second tower. I remember thinking, *Isn't that weird that two planes accidentally hit these towers?* It still didn't sink in. Then the news desk got a call about the Pentagon and the United flight that crashed into a field. It was utter mayhem. At this point our news director just yelled while running across the frantic newsroom, "America is under attack! Stay at your own risk or leave at your own will!" I called my mom and put her on speaker. I briefed her on what was happening and told her to put the news on. She already had it on. Everyone had it on. It was a living horror movie. It still didn't quite sink in that we were under attack. What was supposed to be a regular night, me getting drunk and sleeping with someone I shouldn't have, peanut M&M's, laughing about office gossip, turned upside down into the worst day ever.

People in the newsroom were running back and forth constantly with information that was coming in. The *boom boom* of people running behind you and not looking was jarring. We had to send news crews down to the site ASAP for coverage, and when they finally got down there . . . the buildings collapsed. What I saw next was something I could never unsee. I was looking at small monitors and watching people die. I was watching people. Lots of people taking their last breath. Parents, partners, sons, daughters. I couldn't understand this. Suddenly it hit me how my life was so trivial. All our lives were.

The havoc and destruction that followed after those buildings came down coupled with the knowledge that these were people, innocent people like me who simply showed up for their shifts just like I did. There just aren't any words. I was scared for my safety but felt like I needed to stay. To help anyway I could, to make a difference.

I worked furiously for hours, no bathroom breaks, just looking through a terrible video of a smoking building on a constant loop. I felt a hand on my shoulder, turned around, and it was Beth, who was also an editor. She said, "Go home, you're relieved." I felt like I could just melt onto the floor and take a nap. It was an emotional marathon of go go go, and the minute she said stop, I left. It was 6:00 p.m.

When I got home I called English Muffin. He was grounded and we hung tough, hooked up, and were in just awe with what happened. I don't remember it entirely, I just know I needed to feel something other than grief. I couldn't talk about those next few months for at least seven years. I'd go into editing and work on what felt like a real-life horror movie. One of my jobs was to make one-minute b-roll of the buildings with no bodies jumping from the windows. That was my job. I didn't want to edit these people out. They were already being erased; I didn't want to help with that. My gut was telling me I wasn't cut out for this.

I hung with English Muffin for a few more days before he was able to go back home. We really got to know each other, and it was pretty cute. He was like a low-budget Hugh Grant. A sarcastic English dude that was a lawyer and lived "a bit away" from London because it was "full of drunk knobs."

COURAGE

I was thinking about doing stand-up for a few months before September 11. A lot of coworkers were telling me that I was really funny and that I needed to do stand-up, but I just laughed and said, "Whatever, you cute." I never took them seriously. It's like when you bake a Duncan Hines cake and your friend is like, "You should be on *Great British Baking Show.*" I didn't take them seriously. I don't know why. Maybe I didn't trust myself or think I could do it. It wasn't a dream or goal of mine. I didn't sneak Richard Pryor records up to my bedroom when I was little. I would go to comedy shows from time to time and check it out. It was very male dominated in a way that wasn't inspiring, meaning I never saw a male comedian and thought, *Wow, I love his stuff so much* that I also thought, *Wow, could you not be as sad?* They were all sad, broke, jerking off into dark rooms, avoiding phone calls or any type of connection because God forbid you had a connection. I heard a lot of stand-up comics talk about how broke they were too, and I wasn't ready for all that. I didn't wanna be broke. I worked too hard for my shit. So I was on the fence.

I didn't even realize I had material till I would tell co-workers and friends about my roommate. I had a roommate at the time that had an all-white cat from the street named Cocaine, and I would write emails about Cocaine to my co-workers, and they would forward them to friends because they thought they were so funny. For real, though, that cat was *insane*. One time there was a rat in our bathroom—we thought we were safe because we lived on the second floor but wow, I'll tell ya this, those rats will find their way into their home like it's a ghetto-ass *An American Tail*. My roommate just threw her Cocaine in the bathroom, and those two had it out. It sounded like an MMA fight in Vegas.

I even took a stand-up class to see if this was something I'd be interested in. It was pretty fun, but I was still on the fence. It just seemed like a lot of work for little reward. Then 9/11 happened. Editing video of that horrible afternoon over and over and over again made me think, *Fuck this shit. We're all gonna die; we don't know when or how, so let's get to that back burner of the to-do list of life and make shit happen.* September 14, 2001, I did stand-up for the first time. I fell madly deeply in love with it, and I've been doing it ever since.

THE BIRTHDAY

I had a friend whose birthday is on September 11. I feel bad for people with that birthday because they aren't comfortable celebrating, and I get it. When she turned forty she decided she had to celebrate and hell yes, better! At the time she was a nanny for Angelina Jolie. Angelina hosted a private dinner for her at a chic Tribeca restaurant, and I'm not gonna lie, I was nervous to meet her! My friend prepped me before I went and said, "Whatever you do, please do not tell her that people tell you you look like a Puerto Rican Angelina Jolie."

I said, "That's a great story, no?"

She said, "It's absolutely not a great story. So steer clear."

The dinner was lovely and warm and intimate, but I just couldn't bring myself to make eye contact with Angelina because she can see through your soul and I didn't think I was ready. I overheard Ang (can I call you Ang?) ask my friend, "Who is she?" referring to me! And my friend said, "Oh, my dear friend Michelle; I've known her forever. She's an aspiring stand-up comedian." And Ang said in a disapproving voice,

"Oh, *that* makes sense." WHAT? *WHAT* MAKES SENSE? WHY DOES *THAT* MAKE SENSE?!? Truly one of the greatest mysteries of my life. I don't know what Angelina saw in me that night. Perhaps she saw the truest, most dopest Puerto Rican version of herself.

FISHER-PRICE MY FIRST ROAD GIG

Ask any comic about when they first started doing stand-up and you'll usually find they didn't exactly get *The Tonight Show* within their first couple of months. Comics work hard; it's a fucking grind. When I first started out in 2001 I did a lot of shows in New York City and the outer boroughs. And by "shows" I mean standing in the corner of a bar holding a microphone and trying to compete with seven big-screen TVs showing a Giants playoff game. Nobody was there to watch comedy. I played Laundromats, burger joints, shit, I even did a gig in a church basement. I remember spending so much time in the West Village of New York in basement shows with Amy Schumer, Eric Andre, Hannibal Buress, Michelle Collins, Pete Holmes, and Kumail Nanjiani, to name a few. We were all hustling hard, doing most shows for free. And when I got to do a show at an actual comedy club, I had to earn my place by doing what's called a bringer show. A bringer show is exactly what it sounds like: you bring paying customers to the club, and in return you get five minutes onstage. You do it for experience, a tape of your set perhaps, and most of all, the cache that comes with playing at this club.

I was all about inviting my coworkers at WNBC to my comedy shows. And I did a ton of bringers, so I'd invite all of them.

I heard about doing "the Road." Sounds exciting, doesn't it? "The Road." Ohhhh, where could that lead a bitch? At a jam sesh with Prince? Crowd-surfing in Seattle? Ha! I'll tell you where it leads. Doing gigs in towns you've never heard of that are at least two hours away from the Podunk airport you've landed in. But for the most part, it makes you a better comic in the same way that being cheated on in a relationship makes you a smarter person (if you're lucky). It's a necessary evil, is what I'm trying to say. After maybe two or three years of doing stand-up five or six nights a week, I was hungry to do the Road. I finally got an unlikely invitation after a terrible bar gig where I ended up handing some dude's ass back to him. He yelled out, "Say something funny, bitch!" in the middle of my set. I shot back, "Sir, I hope your dick is as big as your mouth." That's my go-to when any guy heckles me, to make them feel small and stupid for interrupting a working goddess.

Anyway, that back-and-forth killed. So this guy named Vinny or Tito (who fucking knows, I have no memory of shit) invited *me* to Rochester, New York, to perform at a music venue that has comedy shows. He said that they fly you out and put you up, and it's a real show. Finally! And I was going to get paid? Okay, it was only $150, but this was my break! I'm sure most civilians think they know everything there is to know about stand-up because of *The Marvelous Mrs. Maisel*, but that's just not the case.

I landed in the Rochester airport like I was Shakira doing the Super Bowl. I was feeling myself. The feeling you get when someone pays you money for something you've been doing for free is the next level. I hopped in a cab to my hotel only to find out it was a motel. What a difference that one little letter makes. A dingy, old, dilapidated straight-out-of-a-horror-movie motel. I had heard stories about whack conditions on the road. As far as I was concerned, I was going to tell myself this is just part of it. Suck it up. But . . . yuck.

When I walked in everyone looked so ominous like I was Cynthia Erivo in *Bad Times at the El Royale*. (Can I just say that the movie wasn't bad, her voice is butter, and that Chris Hemsworth dude was shirtless a lot in it.) When I checked in, I noticed that the lady at the front desk had a lot of burns on her face. I didn't want to ask, but I was curious.

Then I went in the elevator to go to my room, and I noticed the janitor also had burns on his face, neck, and hands. You have to admit that's a crazy coincidence. For sure they've talked about it to each other. When I was off the elevator, on my floor, walking to my room I felt my chest get tight because this place was so damn dirty. More yuck. Felt like I was in an old thrift shop with dusty old items left by dead people in the garbage. I saw a cleaning lady come out of a room, and guess what? She was a burn survivor too! Okay, now I'm nosy as fuck and have to know the backstory!! What happened? Were they all together? Did they find one another at a support group? Was something going to happen to me? Was I in a haunted hotel on an episode of *American Horror Story*?! It was insane. When I got into my room I was like, *Come on*. Everything looked like it had been straight up on the set of *Psycho*. Ever look into a mirror and feel like someone's staring back at you? Yeah. That's what this felt like. And the view out my window was of a decent hotel.

I really had to work hard to get my shit together because this room was disgusting. It smelled like smoke. There were stains on everything. The comforter looked like someone pulled it out of the garbage, and there was a footprint on it—what? Even the Bible in the side table drawer looked worn. Usually hotel Bibles look like they never get used, so I had a feeling a lot of people had prayed in this creepy place. I was sure there would be two little twin girls waiting to play with me in the hallway, but I pulled my shit together mentally, spiritually, and got ready for the show. I went to the venue early. It was walking distance, so why not. I was insanely early, like hours early. I probably ate a pound of chicken wings and drank one too many cosmos. Look, *Sex and the City* was popular back then and that was the go-to drink for the bishes, what can I say? I'm a simple broad.

Now. I don't know why I fantasized that my first road gig would be at a theater space with maroon curtains and a raised stage. Where I say something so funny that there's a wave of laughter and I just look out into the crowd, waiting for them to stop laughing so I can continue.

This was not that. This show was at a music venue that also looked like a bar you'd see on *Shameless*. A veeeery local watering hole—one you might go to right before you hit rock bottom and head to rehab. At least there was a raised stage, but it also looked like it'd fall apart in two seconds. It reminded me of the stage in *Selena* where she performed in Mexico and people got hurt. (Just a quick apology to my Dutch husband who doesn't ever get any of my references.) The show was hosted by local comics who were really nice. They kept referring to New York City as "the Big City" and "New York Shitty."

It was very obvious that they wanted to go to New York City to do stand-up but they also resented the fact that they never would. I didn't really care either way because the chicken wings were poppin'. Finally the crowd started filing in. People came out for it. Lots of beards and tie-dyed sweatshirts. The room looked like something out of *Fargo*, which I guess is what upstate New York is? I'm no Christopher Columbus! And honestly, the show wasn't bad. My set back then was a very starter-kit comic set. Self-deprecating, "put yourself down and people will like you" kind of stuff. Jokes about being big-boned and how gross subway seats are and how difficult it is to open a door in New York City. Real-life shit. I did well, and it made me forget about my motel room for a few minutes.

After the show, a lady approached me and said I was really funny. She kind of had that first wife from *Sister Wives* vibe: nice and a bit bossy but still caring at the same time. I'm never good at taking compliments but made it one of my resolutions that year to say thank you and keep the fuck moving. She said that she was running a fundraiser after the comedy show but she had terrible stage fright and would I be down to host. I said, "How much?" She said she could give me fifty dollars and pay me in wings. I said, "You've got a deal, lady!" Sweet! I'd be making extra money, and the last thing I wanted to do was go back to the Bates Motel. I asked her what the fundraiser was for and she said the American Stroke Association. Dope! Look at me out here doing comedy for good causes. Michelle Buteau: American comedian and philanthropist . . .

When I got backstage I noticed a bunch of men oiling their chests up and slapping their dicks awake. I asked her, what dis? She said it's a male strip revue! Get it? American Stroke Association? Ew, I get it, I got it, I don't want it. But okay, fine. Anything besides the Bates Motel. The problem was I didn't know anything about hosting a comedy show, let alone a low-budget, Middle America, Magic Mike session, but there we were, folks. When it comes to comedy you just have to say yes to everything in order to get good at it. And this was one of those times.

I took comedy pretty seriously and wanted to do a good job no matter what the caliber of show. I was the only female on the show and if I had an off day, people might leave the room thinking women aren't funny. It's a sad but true fact every female comic faces at one point or another, so you have to represent. I went up to each "performer"—okay—stripper and asked them what their credits were, what they wanted me to say about them. I thought I'd be like a big-tittied Nick Cannon hosting *America's Got Talent*. I would be presenting these dancers-turned-strippers, and here we go.

I imagined saying, "My next performer got his start when he was on the high school jazz team. You can catch him at the local theater doing *Mamma Mia!* . . ." Instead they gave me, "Ladies, is your kitty cat missing? 'Cause we've got a pet detective on the case." I had to go around the whole room, the whole dumb room, getting proper introductions from male strippers performing at a rock club in Rochester, New York, whose claim to fame is hot wings. I was making it, for sure.

The first guy to perform was named Papi. I said, "What's your real name?"

He said his real name was Papi.

I said, "Why'd your mom name you Papi?"

He said, "Because when I was born my mother said I looked like my dad." (I was praying his sister looked like their mother.) The crowd had changed over from a mix of local men and women to all women. Housewives, single chicks, gym teachers, tollbooth workers with single dollar bills in their hands, screaming at the top of their vaginas, hungry for the D.

I got onstage and said, "Hi, ladies," and it was like a group of teenagers just saw the Beatles for the first time. Ha, my references are so old. Okay, it's like a bunch of teenagers just saw Harry Styles for the first time! I immediately felt a rush go through my body. Oh shit, I had these bitches in the palm of my hand. They wanted to be there so bad. I don't know what came over me. I had a dumbtastic opener ready to go, and instead I just yelled, "Y'all ready to see some DICCCCCKKKKKKK?" I really wish you could've been there. To see these housewives lose their fucking minds with their minivan keys attached to their purses and all their kids' lunch money in their hands, ready to rock and roll. They were screaming so loud they looked like the pileup scene of zombies in *World War Z*. If those zombies were really fucking horny.

"Our first exotic dancer you can see at the Village Gate Square mall. This is also his debut appearance! He's looking for a mami; please welcome Papi!" Papi then comes out and dances to "Motown Philly" in his civilian clothing. He didn't even have a costume. It was sad and hilarious and back to sad and just a big what the faaack. You had to admire his courage but also wonder if he was okay. He had on baggy jeans and a Tommy Hilfiger polo. Before you act like this is 1995, it wasn't, it was 2003! Which I'm only realizing now is not that far off from 1995. Papi danced around the long picnic tables while ladies just yelled at him to take it off, but they weren't giving him any money. As he peeled his jeans off, he revealed that he had on boxers. What? Um. Okay. Then he took off those boxers only to reveal . . . another pair of boxers. Oh, okay. He thought about this. Poor, poor Papi. He took off those boxers that revealed—wait for it—ANOTHER PAIR OF FUCKING BOXERS. I think he put the whole pack on. I had so many emotions I didn't know how to compute. They weren't even nice boxers; they looked used and washed. I could tell it was his grand finale, and yes, please make it end. He was doing a lot of jackhammer dancing with his eyes closed, and it looked like he was making a wish and blowing out the candles. He was actually making me hungry for cake.

Papi climbed up onstage and slowly took off his boxers. The PTA meeting was still into whatever bullshit he was selling, and I just couldn't believe what I was watching. When he peeled his last boxer off he had on tighty-whities. Tight-ass white underwear on and when he bent over there. It. Was. A. Fucking. Stain. A simple brown stain that will be forever on my brain. The ladies were clapping and into it. But I think the tables in the front were the only ones that saw the skid marks, so his big finale was met with mostly applause and a few groans and ewwws.

"Give it up for Papi, everyone, let him hear you. He just served us Russian doll realness with that boxers trick. There's no one else like him and thank God for that. He says if you need a leather jacket at Wilsons mention this show and he'll give you ten percent off. Up next, I don't know who's afraid of the dentist, but Justin would love to make you feel comfortable while he drills your holes." Yes, that was the intro he gave me—which I believe I repeated back to him for confirmation.

This was Fisher-Price My First Road Gig, but this was also the American Stroke Association Fisher-Pricing, because who the fuck fantasizes about a sexy dentist? We fantasize about a dentist who doesn't charge two thousand dollars for one crown. This dude came out to "Footloose," rocking a white lab coat. And I don't know if the idea was to mimic a dental drill but he just started spinning. And he did a bunch! He spun so much I got dizzy watching him. Shit, he spun so much I could tell he got dizzy. That was his signature move, spinning? That's a terrible signature move! That's like a taxi driver's signature move being stepping on the brakes every five seconds. That's just awful. He looked like he was the kid that would do his *SNL* audition in the bathroom mirror, a lot. I just knew he had an Adam Sandler impersonation in that lab coat pocket. He wasn't *not* attractive. He had a Leo DiCaprio vibe with the forehead of Dawson's Creek. (Ha, go with me.) But I couldn't tell if he was attractive or not because he just kept spinning. I felt like he had something to hide. "Footloose" is about four minutes long. That's so long. When he'd stop spinning he'd stand in place, have his hands on his head, and do a circle motion with his head and then his groin. Not sure how he'd do in the sheets, but for sure my teeth would be clean.

(Off script.) "Wow. Give it up for Dr. Justin! He spun us right round round round like a record, baby!" (Silence, then back to script.) "Ladies, hold on to your purses." And cue some kind of weird setup where the only Black dude in the whole building runs out into the showroom to no music pretending as if he's stolen a purse. (He was probably the dude making the wings in the back.) He came running through the tables full of soccer moms with a hooded sweatshirt on, holding a tiny purse. He played his part up a little too well because the women were into it, but he kept going on and on, and then they started saying, "Is it real?!"

I just decided to stick to the script. That's the thing when you first start stand-up, you stick to the script. You don't know enough or feel completely comfortable enough to have license to go off and do whatever you think the room needs. That takes time, to be comfortable. I can't say how long it took for me to be comfortable, but I do know it's when you stop caring about what people think. That's when you can do your best work. So I just read the next thing I was supposed to read, "Ladies, what's going on in your neighborhood? Someone called nine-one-one and Officer Friendly is here and he wants to patrol your home with his nightstick." What the fuck? I went to college. In a different state. I passed my driver's license on the first try. I have freckles. I have so much going for me. But here I am, with buffalo-sauce-stained fingernails reading this shit to *Housekeeping Magazine Presents: Moms Gone Wild.*

"Officer Friendly" came out in his Party City policeman uniform that looked like it was made of paper. His nightstick was a black plastic bat. He was attractive from what I remember. He looked like Pauly D from *Jersey Shore*. He had very stiff hair and looked like he hit the gym and drank his whey protein shakes every day. Commitment: that's what I remember from this guy. He came out and spun that stick like he was in a Miss America contest and his talent was baton. No, seriously. He twirled it up. He twirled it down. He twirled it all around. He humped it a little bit. He seductively suggested it was the size of his dick, and honestly it could've been because it was an underwhelming plastic fucking baton. At first I was just salty: he had the audacity of hope to come out here and dance with a dollar-store prop? But he danced *so hard* with this baton, making it his only focus, I couldn't stop watching. I was just sucked in. He danced with that baton like he was going for a ten on *Dancing with the Stars*. The ladies could feel his energy too. They went from throwing one-dollar bills to *five* dollars. Damn. I knew this candle party gone wrong was about that life when I saw the five-dollar bills!! How are your kids gonna pay for their lunch this week, ladies? His song, "I'm Gonna Get You," has the lyrics "Why waste your time, you know you're gonna be mine!" And ya know? I was his. I didn't have any cash, but if I did I'd throw it at his dumb face because he won me over. The commitment and utter joy that ensued from this man that didn't even have a real costume was unlike any I'd ever seen. He didn't care that we were in a dive venue that smelled like bleach, stale beer, and Frank's hot sauce. He wasn't fazed at all that he had on a costume that was made from cheap, highly flammable synthetic materials. He gave zero fucks that he had to work a room of premenopausal *Golden Girls* fans with a plastic nunchuck. He *did* that shit.

There's a few rules in comedy. One is to go where you're the worst comic and follow someone who's funnier than you, and another is don't steal other people's shit. Officer Friendly showed me something else important. He taught me how to have unbridled joy in what I was doing no matter the circumstances. That while you're onstage it's your job to bring people into your world, and don't take no for an answer.

I went back to my motel room and did some gentle rocking on a safe part of the bed to try to soothe myself, but it wasn't working. So I went to the airport early. Very early. Like, behind the TSA in line at Dunkin' Donuts early. When I got home I felt exhausted and forever changed. I don't know of any other job that would take you on such a journey. The first thing I did was tell everyone what the fuck happened, and nobody believed me. Then I donated fifty dollars to the actual American Stroke Association.

People often ask me if they can pick my brain over coffee, to help them figure out how to get into comedy. There's no way to figure out this crazy occupation. You have to say yes to everything for a good while; you'll know when you have to start saying no. You have to put yourself in the most awkward, unstable situations to get so comfortable onstage that, by the time you get to the big stage, it'll feel like nothing for you. It'll feel so comfortable you'll just be surprised that you're performing in a room conducive to comedy. No spinning, no plastic batons; unless the money is right.

SURVIVAL OF THE THICKEST

According to Dictionary.com, *the prime of your life* means "the best years of one's life, when one is at the peak of one's powers." But for most women, that translates to "the time when they were thin and beautiful." This is something my mother talks about nonstop when she sees old pictures of herself. "Meh wish meh new'ow prettay en ting meh' was." When I look at old pictures of myself, I realize, I've spent a lot of time waiting for my prime.

I never looked like my mom growing up. She was thin, with wavy hair (she's half white). She could wear bikinis and miniskirts as the day is long. I never had that. I've always been an odd-body. I try to keep my shirts tucked in, but somehow they always find a way out. I have learned to be comfortable just sitting with a wedgie. I always have a wedgie. Cloth just finds its way in my holes. Like a chimney that's closed, the smoke has to go somewhere—and that's usually my butt. Clothes dig into my nooks and crannies and try to hide like Harrison Ford in *The Fugitive*. I swear, I'm such a mess that if I watch other people eat, somehow I'll get their food on my shirt. If I watch someone else eat like a pig, I'll be five pounds heavier the next morning. I wanna reclaim my prime like Auntie Maxine Waters wants to reclaim her time at a hearing: "Reclaiming my prime! Reclaiming my prime!"

My prime is having breath in my body and pep in my step. My prime is that I'm a dope wife, a present mother, a caring friend, and a funny-ass woke bitch onstage. My prime is that I wake up every day and have a cute choice in wardrobe—because the fashion industry has either decided that as a size 18 broad I'm worthy of style, or perhaps they just want to make a buck off my booty. Who knows? I'll think about it when I put on my ripped jeans and off-the-shoulder sweatshirt.

When I turned twelve what I wanted for my birthday was a new bike. An iridescent purple banana-seat bike with glitter tassels on the handlebars. What I got was a set of workingwoman-size tits. No, for real. I went to bed as an eleven-year-old with an eleven-year-old body, then I woke up the next day with huge tits. It was like an NC-17 version of *Big* with Tom Hanks, but my reboot would be called *Thick* with Michelle Buteau.

I didn't want these tits, but what was I gonna do? They didn't come with a gift receipt, so I had to be on my merry way with them. In most families, women pass down recipes. In my family, women pass down big-ass titties. Instead of inheriting millions of dollars, I got triple Ds and an E. What followed that year was even more confusing than an overnight growth spurt.

I had to deal with my prime-time-thin perfect mother telling me to "Stop stickin' ya breasts owt gehl!" I was wearing the same exact clothes I'd always worn before tittypocolypse. Now I'm being shamed for having good posture? CONFUSING.

Ya see, I wasn't mature enough to stick up for myself. After all, this is my mom. I didn't even know I was being shamed by the lady that should be protecting me. I truly thought this is just what moms do. "Clean up your room. Stop sticking out your chest." But wow, looking back on it, I wish the woman—or at least the mother—had told me that it'd be okay, that'd I'd grow into my body. I wish she'd helped me find clothes so I could express myself like everyone else in school.

Back then there weren't any plus-size clothing options. I know I'm aging myself but truly, the nineties are considered back in the day. And back in the day, the only garments you could find that could fit over tight ol' biddies were older-lady office wear or men's clothing. So what's a seventh grader to choose? Mrs. Doubtfire or Pat from *SNL*? (Please google if under thirty-eight.)

There were a lot of times where I'd sneak into my father's closet and steal his button-down office shirts. One time I even rocked one of his ties like a Puerto Rican Ellen DeGeneres. He still talks about a three hundred dollar shirt I borrowed to wear to a party in eighth grade. Dad, if you're reading this, you have to get over it, man.

As a young girl with woman-size tits I'd get so much unwanted attention from older men it was gross. I was still playing with Barbies and video games and then I'd walk down the street to go to the 7-Eleven to get Twizzlers, and old guys would try to flirt with me. The thing that really bothered me is that my mom would blame me. My dad on the other hand would tell these guys where to go and how to get there and it wasn't pleasant, but at least I felt stood up for.

My mother had big tits, too, so if anything I thought we'd be able to commiserate over this bullshit. But no. By the time I got to ninth grade baggy street clothes were in, and thank the Lord Jesus Christ and His disciples. That's the only way I could've dressed myself in the nineties without looking like Dorothy from Golden Girls, so I'm thankful for my Cross Colour shirts that came down to my knees—and that everyone else dressed exactly the same.

I looked so mature for my age it was weird. One time I went back-to-school shopping for supplies at Kmart and a woman asked me if I knew where to find the Trapper Keepers. Say what now? I knew where they were but that's not the fucking point. I wasn't even a certified teenager and I looked so old she thought that I worked there? It's hard looking that mature because people think you're supposed to act mature. No one else in my grade had huge voluptuous breasts and hips except the teachers, and even they weren't as thick as me.

Going to an all-white Catholic school didn't help. You would think uniforms would be of service, but nope! My uniform didn't look like everyone else's. The button that lay on my boobs looked like the boat in *Life of Pi*, just hanging on by a thread. I wasn't fat, but since I was bigger than everyone else, I was made to feel fat, called fat, believed I was fat, and that fat was a bad thing.

My cousin told me the other day that I was the only eighth grader he knew that did sit-ups. I don't remember that, but how sad is that shit? I should be worrying about what Bobby Brown is going to do on the red carpet at the Grammys or what hair ties to put in my Caboodle #vintage #reference, not why is my stomach too big and why does my uniform skirt go up in the back? Why do I have a "shelf booty" before I can even reach shit off an actual shelf?

If you grew up with a body that you weren't comfortable in, then you understand. Yes, it's an awkward age, but no one ever talks about it. You're just supposed to deal with the cards you've been given and be thankful that you're healthy. Other thirteen-year-old girls had barely sprouted, and I looked like I was breastfeeding the whole eighth-grade class.

On to bathing suit shopping. Wow, I'd rather go to the dentist and get four root canals without anesthesia than go bathing suit shopping as a preteen in an adult body.

Every year television and magazine covers were screaming at me, "Get that summer bikini body by spring or else ya fucked!" "Work off that flab so you can look fab or else ya fucked!" No one was hammering into my mind "Be happy, Michelle! You can do and be whoever you want! Little girls can be president too!" Nope, that's never the fucking message. It was just triple Bs: bikini body, bitch.

I have a conspiracy theory that bathing suits are purposefully designed to make women look bigger physically and feel smaller emotionally. Pool parties were huge growing up in the burbs, and all that meant was me giving myself an ulcer.

Yet there are actually women out there who effortlessly just put on a bathing suit and "can't decide which one to wear because they all look so cute!" The only anxiety they have is picking the one with cherries on it or the one with stripes.

I hate, hate, will always loathe being in a fitting room with all these pieces of fabric on a hanger that I know won't fit. When I was young, I hated that I had to go in public and pretend to be comfortable when I know that everyone's looking at how developed my body is. I wish I had Amazon back then. And you know what's fucked-up? What's truly fucked and stupid? For a good significant while I really did think I was less of a woman if I couldn't wear a bikini.

Whenever there was a dressy occasion I would give myself another ulcer because there weren't any stores for young women of a certain weight. And holy fuck, what was I gonna wear? There was nothing out there for me. Everything that fit my body would make me look like a grown-ass woman. I didn't want to look like a woman; I wanted to look my age. I wanted to look like a tween. I never have.

My mother just ended up dressing me in a lot of black. I could have easily passed for an Italian, Greek, or perhaps Puerto Rican widow. To be a size 12 when you are twelve, it's pretty wild. When I was six I used to put my mom's shoes on and play dress-up. In a few short years I was bigger than her, bigger than most people in my family. They gave me a lot of shit for it.

Going to college in Miami was the first time I felt free to embrace my curves. I was pretty excited to be around other Caribbean people, especially women that looked like me. Everyone has a booty and a gut and big, thick titties and shit, where we shopping, everyone? Oh snap! Sears has an XL? Well, look at these cute-ass maxi dresses at this Walmart. Sure, most of the people shopping here don't have shoes on and the soles of their feet are black—barf, yuck, no, but oh snap! This dress doesn't have a size but fits my body and it comes with the hanger! Walmart, Target, Old Navy, Macy's, Sears. These shops made me FEEL worthy. To this day, I can't go to a boutique to shop.

If a shop somewhere in Beverly Hills or SoHo has four racks of clothes, I'm walking right past them. They do not cater to real bodies. I didn't know that at first. I would see a cute store that was open and ask, "Do you have this in a twelve?" They'd say, "Sorry," and look me up and down like I'm Julia Roberts's character in *Pretty Woman*. Only in this case the "Big Mistake! Huge!" line was referring to anyone over a size 6. Sometimes I'll go to a boutique place with friends and hang out while they shop. I'll buy perfume or jewelry 'cause those things always fit.

People treat you differently if you're a bigger person.

It's just a fact. Having big boobs is like rocking a super-short haircut (hear me out): You have to dress around them. You can't just put something on and do you. If a part of your boob is slightly sticking out like titty meat, then men think, *She wants it*, and women think, *What a whore*. When you're bigger in general, people look at you like it's your fault. Like there's something wrong with you. That you're lazy or you eat too much or you don't like yourself. Men don't hold the door open for you. Walking down the street or in a club and a guy would try to holler, and I'd ignore them or say nah, and they'd say "Fuck you, bitch, you're fat anyway." How did we go all the way there?

What really sucks is when you're put down by someone who's supposed to lift you up. I remember going to college and wanting to be a journalist. Okay, an entertainment reporter. It looked like a lot of fun. People pay you to go to the movies and talk about it on camera, what a dream! Then I told one of my professors that and he plainly and simply told me (in front of the whole class) that I was too fat to be on camera. This was in 1996, when no one questioned authority, especially the students. There was no protest, no hashtag available. And I think about that day all the time. I believe I'm a late bloomer because of it. I went into TV production instead of studying to be on-camera talent. I could kick myself in the butt for believing him, but that's how I was raised: be polite, don't question authority.

I often think of who I could be if I had told him to fuck

off and just did my thing, but that's not my truth. I worked my ass off in TV production, and for years people in the business told me I needed to be on camera and then I finally did it. There's no right or wrong way to get to where you want to get to as long as you fucking get there. But who the fuck was he to say that to a young, burgeoning mind? And why did I believe it? I'm sure people told Obama he'd never be president because he was Black. Or Oprah she couldn't be successful because she was Black and a woman. AHHH!!!! How dare he tell a young woman that she cannot do something because of her size. I think about him all the time. Too much, to be honest. I hope he's still alive and has Netflix and is just rewinding all my scenes in everything I've done and feels bad about his bullshit. I highly doubt it though.

After college my boobs just kept getting bigger. One was a triple D and the other was an E. I was uncomfortable and it was hard to do anything. Sit, stand, walk, dance. I had to wear a bra to bed. It was crazy exhausting. I was naturally a happy person, but it was harder and harder to find joy. My mother would always tell me that my boobs were too big. She'd say it in a way where there was disdain in her voice. As if I chose this. Of course you don't want to disappoint your mother, but what if you literally just woke up and she got mad at your face? That's what that felt like. And, PS—I inherited these, memba dat?

My dad introduced the idea of a breast reduction to me. He's a real one. He's one of those cuts-through-the-bullshit kinda guys. If he asks a question, it's because he wants to know. He doesn't care for polite talk; he believes that is for lesser beings. (I know, I KNOW.) My dad said, "You don't look happy or comfortable, and you are the type of person that needs to be happy and comfortable. One time you joked and said your bra is the stuff bridges are made of. That was sad. Let's look into a breast reduction." And that was that.

I didn't know what to make of it. Hell, I don't like when I get my cuticles cut, so obviously this scared the shit out of me. But I did some research (truly Google had just come out), so I was interested. My mother was vehemently against it. She said "Metchelle, You don't go uhndah dee knife unless you 'af to." But of course I "'af to!!" I'm the equivalent of one of those women on *The Howard Stern Show* who can crush beer cans with their tits. My tits are so big #howbigarethey I can smuggle sixty-five pounds under them. And they were going *National Geographic* at this point. They never grew out, they just grew down. Half of my tit was just areola.

When I'd make out with my college boyfriend he had to lift my tit up in order to find my nipple to suck on it. To be honest, when he hoisted these fleshy sandbags up, my shoulders finally stopped hurting! At that point I wondered if I'd ever make enough money to have someone just hold my tits up for me. I went to this downtown trendy Miami doctor for a consultation. My father came with me for support. My mother wanted nothing to do with it. I told the front desk receptionist that I was interested in breast augmentation because that's what I thought it was called. She looked at me sideways. Great, she has an attitude. Whoops! I thought *augment* was just to change something but it in fact means to make something bigger! Could you imagine what this poor woman was thinking? She probably assumed I was there to donate.

I ended up getting a breast reduction, and it's the best thing that could have ever happened. Insurance didn't cover it because I was too tall and too heavy to qualify for whatever bullshit rules applied, so we had to pay out of pocket. I couldn't have thanked my dad enough. I don't remember how much it was, but it was truly a priceless gift. I was in pain for a few weeks because boobs are just so sensitive, but I was able to see my feet, and that was amazing. I really think Dolly Parton is the only person that can pull off boobs like that. They're just so cumbersome. I'll never forget the day I strapped on two exercise bras and just went jogging. It was amazing. I felt like I was free in a way that I hadn't been since before puberty.

I threw a ball! I clapped my hands! All without some serious struggle. I felt like a new person. I lost about twenty pounds after my breast reduction, broke up with my college boyfriend, and decided to move to New York City with a new wardrobe and outlook. I still struggled with my weight. I'd gain and lose and gain and lose. It's always been a fight to figure out what a healthy goal is.

Thick means that you've got meat on your bones, bitch,

and there's nothing wrong with that. I am thick. Yet I have thick friends who'd always make fun of me and tell me that I'm not big at all and shut up about being a big girl. Then I'd have pint-size friends who'd tell me "You're not that big!" Well, bitch, which is it? I swear people made me feel like my body is the middle seat on an airplane. It's not ideal, and some people will take it if they have no choice, but most don't prefer it. I would go into packed bars, and my body parts would gently glide up on people. Yuck. I kept seeing pictures of myself and didn't recognize that person. I'd force people into a group pic just so I could hide myself behind a wall of skinnier bodies. It wasn't fun. And I love to have fun; I am fun. I didn't have money for a trainer. I was living on the Upper West Side in New York City, and I couldn't even afford the Lululemon pants that most of the ladies in my neighborhood would wear. I tried the vintage approach, working out by myself with a DVD player. But there's something so depressing about throwing air punches at your television by yourself, like you're fighting a ghost.

I really wanted to go to the gym, but I didn't want to look stupid if I didn't know how to work the machines. I don't know how to put together an IKEA bookshelf, let alone turn on the StairMaster at the gym. And I've tried all the gyms. I never wanted to commit, so I did a trial run at six gyms, which got me six free weeks of going to the gym for one day. Signing up for a gym feels like you're at a Jiffy Lube that is about to close down and they're trying to upsell you on everything. A place like Equinox charges more than your rent so you can have lavender-scented towels and can waddle behind the group class instructors who are all professional backup dancers for Madonna. (True story.) The other option is the cheap gym. They get you on their low introductory price. Then you show up and it looks like the outdoor recreation prison facility in *American History X*. I was completely frustrated with all the gym nonsense, but I still wanted to work the fuck out and live my best life, like Oprah on an upswing. This woman is a powerhouse, a billionaire, one of the most well-known women in the world, and yet she still struggles with fettuccine—and I love that about her.

Of course I wanted to write bits about gyms for my act, and I was running a joke by my comedy buddy Dan. He suggested we comics stop running jokes and actually start running together. Aaaaand cue another ulcer. Do I really wanna work out in public? With these tits? With people who get paid to make fun of other people professionally? I said yes to the dress though. I mean, what did I have to lose? It was free, and I was going to be in the company of people I knew. A safe space before we invented safe spaces. Half these muthafuckers are smokers, so hopefully that's an advantage for me.

I showed up one Tuesday morning in my tired-ass workout yoga pants from college. Good thing was I wasn't the only one wearing terrible workout clothes. One comedian had ripped shorts on, another had on three old exercise bras that barely combined into one. Dan made us all stretch in his living room and passed around a joint right as we were about to leave. Apparently when he was in college he belonged to a running club called "5K BHC," or Bong Hit Club. You run a 5K (which is about three miles) high and/or run sober and get high after. The point is, you gotta get high. I'm terrible at being high. I want to think I'm cool as fuq, spitting poetry and lyrics for people's minds to explode with flavor, like a low-budget Erykah Badu but I'm an Erykah Ba-Don't. #sorrynotsorry.

I got high, coughed my little old lungs out, and charged out with my crazy piecemeal crew of adults in pajamas and old sneakers. Our fearless, stoned leader, Dan, had planned a perfect 5K loop around Central Park, and it felt like I was in *National Lampoon's Vacation.* Everyone kept complaining and whining about how out of shape they were, how terrible gyms were, and I'm like, *Holy fuck, my people!* We started with a light jog and the next thing you know we're all running at weird different paces like we're chasing bulls on a crowded street in the south of Spain. Everyone was talking shit about one another and other people running past us and it was hysterical. Picture running outside with the less successful Chris Rock, Jeff Ross, and Lisa Lampanelli. Our one friend's shorts are flapping in the wind, holding on for dear life. He's starting to chafe. I'm so high I can't stop laughing, and I'm running and holding on to my breasts like two Chihuahuas fighting in a BabyBjörn.

Three miles can seem really daunting when you have

never done it. Then you finally do it and it's like getting your ears pierced or riding a roller coaster or anal—it's over before you know it! We were all so proud of ourselves we decided to get Mexican brunch and undo everything we just accomplished. And that's how you maintain chunky. That's how you work out to fit into your workout clothes.

It was so fun that we did it every weekend for the next two months. We were feeling ourselves so hard, we were like, *Why don't we meet up during the week too?* This became my all-in-one hang. While we were running we'd all talk about our problems: What comic was mean to us? What comedy club won't put me up? How should I text this guy back? How do you finish this joke? It was cardio-therapy. It was also a great way to learn how to get high and still be productive.

I could definitely feel my body getting stronger. I'm no Dr. Oz but I thought, What would happen if I stopped eating all that Mexican food right after running? OMG it was like Transformation Tuesdays on Hoda and Kathie Lee. Everyone knows that you're supposed to eat right and exercise to get healthy, but that felt like too much at one time.

Dan got engaged and he wanted to up the runs and lose more weight. We were all in. We worked hard. Didn't get high first. We did the damn thing. Sometimes we ran even longer than three miles. This is when I realized, if you want to lose weight and get in shape? TIP #18: Workout with a friend who is getting married. (I don't know what the first seventeen tips are.) Working out is the only thing they want to do. You'll be on their journey with them and end up looking amazing! We signed up for half marathons and started traveling to different cities to run them. We were obsessed.

Those medals from the marathons are still some of my greatest accomplishments. From being scared to go to the gym by myself, to walking proudly into Target and buying workout clothes to use them and loving cardio? That's dope. Most people will say a great workout tip is having someone to rely on, then you'll show up. I don't know how true that is. I don't mind canceling at all, and I've got no qualms about it. Shit, every year I file for a tax extension 'cause I can't get it together for the government.

I believe I succeeded because I was just very unhappy and needed to do something about it. You can't beat yourself up for not getting there right away; it'll take time. It's not all about the physical. You have to wrap your mind around doing something outside of your comfort zone and perhaps looking stupid. If you're unhealthy, overweight, and unhappy with the way you look, take a good look at yourself in mirror. Have an honest chat about what your goals are no matter how small or big, and just try. You'll be a better person for it, I promise!

I moved to Los Angeles, and I knew that my weight would be a thing. I just didn't know how it would really affect me trying to work there. Everyone in LA treats their body like a temple. I learned if you have an extra ten-plus pounds on your temple, you are officially a character actor. And what that means is you'll be the best friend the skinny girl confides in. That seems like a lot of tap-dancing for a part that isn't going to go anywhere. After auditioning lots in LA I realized that thick women are always auditioning to play the best friend, and even that shit gets competitive. So I could either go in for character roles or Black roles.

Black girl auditions in Los Angeles are the best—it feels like a sassy tailgate at the Super Bowl. We'd sit around and catch up. In the waiting room actors don't talk to one another because everyone's competing, but we had it figured out. If one of us made it, we'd all make it. Gotta pave the way and make being a Black woman with an opinion acceptable. I've been on brown-titty auditions where girls are exchanging recipes, giving plant-care advice—shit, I've even been on Black Girl Magic auditions where they've made a prayer circle. It's a dream. Usually on auditions people look at you like you're shit on their shoes . . . but when you go out on big-girl auditions it's the opposite. We're all out here just so thankful that someone has written a part for us.

Then there's the auditions where they mention they are "open to diversity," which means it's a wild card. The wild card could mean anything. It's Asian, Indian, Spanish, gay, Black, other, etc. Usually "other" would get it. Those are the most popular auditions too.

Everyone is so hard on themselves. People always complain about their problem areas: my gut is a problem area; my chin is a problem area; I don't have thigh gap. Who gives a shit? Honestly, why do we have to call these areas problems? I call them human areas. Yeah, this is human as fuck. I just did three rounds of IVF and got this back fat from the hormone injections. I'm a shero. This back fat is my human area. We spend enough time beating ourselves up, we don't have to talk shit about an area on our body that is actually functioning. Let's not be so mean.

When I started booking jobs as the sassy tell-it-like-it-is neighbor person, I noticed how everyone would eat on set. The people that were the leads always had green stuff on their plate and a juice and no coffee but green tea and cashews for a snack. They were always hyperaware of what they put in their mouth. I'm not mad at it. I'm not shaming people for being conscious of what they eat—you need to; I get it. But it was all so regimented that there was no joy for food or flavor or taste. I would hang out with these actors and they were pretty skinny, and every time they ate something they'd say, "Oh my God, I'm so fat I have to run like a mile to get this off." Wow, I'm not very good at math and never think that way. Why would you? It's exhausting. My favorite part of traveling is that you get to taste food made in other places. See how people celebrate being around a table together. I could never get on board with eating five pieces of dried mango and beating myself up over it. I also didn't want to be the only female getting the lasagna at lunch and deal with the judgy eyes. So I would put pasta on my plate and then cover it with lots of salad. What can I say? I've got lots of tricks to avoid confrontation with any low-budget Jillian Michaels.

I remember when I was little watching TV thinking, "Hmmm nobody looks like me." There were Black people. Light-skin Black folks, all that shit. But no one had boobs, a real figure, curves. Finally Mrs. Delta Burke gained weight on *Designing Women*, and I remember thinking, *Wow, that's pretty badass*. I was really young. And she was so beautiful to me. Then she was body-shamed so badly there was a part of me that thought, *Well I guess they had to do that because she's on camera and being skinny is her job*. Aretha Franklin was a "thickums," and I remember my aunts talking about how she never had control of her weight and that she had a husband who wanted her to be big so no one else would steal her. What in the actual fuck? First of all, is that a thing? Second, she's the gaht damn Queen of Soul, let this woman have her oxtail and hush puppies if she wants!

At the end of the day, people love to shame big girls for wearing bathing suits and being proud of their bodies. They'll never change so let them. Big girls are all about having personal pride. You can and should be proud of your body. I've learned just because I don't fit the basic patriarchal idea of what a woman should look like doesn't mean that I am not worthy of love or sex or attention or to wear something and feel fucking pretty. For years and years and years I've tried to make my body into the unrealistic standard of beauty that Western culture has created. Everyone is different, and we're never going to look the same. And that's okay. I got to see Obama as president, Tess Holliday on the cover of magazines, and Lizzo twerking at the MTV Music Awards.

I'm giving a big titty-to-titty bear hug to that eleven-year-old, thick, mixed chick with the freckled face, and I'm telling her, "Be happy, Michelle!! You can do and be whomever you want."

MY HOLLAND TUNNEL

BEST NIGHT EVER

The joint was called Bembe, and I loved it. I could even hang out by myself and everything was cool. It was wall-to-wall dreads, linen tank tops, and overpriced "cash only" guava drinks, coupled with the sounds of world music and drums. It was my spot. I could spin or be spun. It didn't matter. I was having fun. Pretty soon, a cute dude with a hat asked me to dance. But he had nice shoes and good breath and this hat. Hat-boy keeps spinning me and spinning me and spinning me, until I ghosted him right out the back door and into a taxi. I had fun but was tired, my pinky toes had little hearts in them, and it was time. But homeboy chases me out and sticks his head in the taxi window.

"I'm going with you," he says.

"Oh no, you're not. I'm not that kind of girl," I said. (LOL come on bish.)

So I whipped out my MISHY B: ACTRESS, COMEDIAN, WRITER, PRODUCER business card because, you know, I be hustlin'. And I said, "Here's my card. Call me." It felt like I was the Black girl in 9 to 5 or was it Working Girl? Oh, wait. There are no Black girls in either of those. Sigh, but you get it. I was werking and ghosting and throwing the ball into his court.

The next day, he called. We met for coffee, which turned into tequila. He was in town from Holland and was leaving the next morning. After a few hours of flirty, Rosetta Stone–type chitchat I said, "You gonna kiss me or what?" He was taken aback, but if there's one thing about us Jersey gurls, we know what we want, so he kissed me, and hear me out—this is weird—I fell in love. I could tell he was a good person. I could tell right away from that first kiss that we could have a bond and take care of each other. But we just had some drinks, a handful of dances, I knew nothing would come of it. I had a long weekend doing shows, so I invited him to hang out in my hood (lol do de math) and that's what he did. He hung out in my neighborhood that night. And left to go back home in the morning.

THE LONGEST DISTANCE

When Dutchy (his name is Gijs. It's so Dutch. Uncut Dutch.) went home I thought I'd never hear from him again. And why should I? We had a great night, and he was on vacation. I know how these things go. I've seen *Two Night Stand* and *Night Owls*; I've been on vacation; I live in New York City; I get it. What I didn't expect was a text from him telling me he got home safe. Um, that's so cute? Too cute. Bye, boy; boy, bye.

Then he followed up with, *How are you doing?*

Girl, I'm good, I'm out here hustling trying to make this paper and keep this cable on.

He thought everything I said was funny. That's important, especially for an up-and-coming comedian. Yes, please laugh and be amused, it's all I've got!

We exchanged text messages for a couple of days, and then about a week later he sent me a picture that he took of us in bed. The subject of the email was "Put This on Your Website." But my boob was hanging out a little. So I replied, "I can't, my boob is hanging out." Then he sent me back a picture where my boob was photoshopped out and he put a mustache on me. I don't know why I thought that was the funniest shit ever, but I did. I thought it was just the right amount of sass. Which if I ever have a perfume line, that'll be the name of it.

We started casually emailing each other, and that turned into Gchatting, and that soon turned into phone calls. I don't know what it was about him; it was just easy and fun. I remember canceling some stand-up comedy shows so I could be home on the phone with him. We'd always end up falling asleep on the phone. It was too much! We both were broke artists and had no idea how we'd see each other again. He was an up-and-coming photographer who worked as a photographer's assistant, and I was on my stand-up grind trying to start headlining. He begged me to come to Amsterdam to visit him, but I'd been listening to a lot of Destiny's Child that month and told him my mantra: "I don't take trips to see a boy I take trips to meet boys." What the fuck was I talking about? Here is a cute boy, a nice guy, he's decent and wants to spend time with me, and I say some shit like that? Maybe I was playing hard to get. Maybe I was just protecting myself. You can't get hurt if you're not available. But how are you supposed to find love if you're never available?

A few months had passed by, and we were still talking every day, all the time, first thing and last call of the day. It had gotten pretty intense in all the right ways, but we still had no plans to see each other. While he was taking photos for a job, a sneaker shoot in the street where streets are old and small, a cop ran over his foot by accident, breaking his ankle. What in the natural fuck? So he really couldn't afford to travel to see me. I was performing at the Bonnaroo Music and Arts Festival in bumble-fuck Tennessee, opening up for Louis C.K. and Jim Norton—oh yeah, the audience was very female-forward—when I got a video file from Gijs. It took me almost two days to figure out how to open it. It was a five-minute video that he made for me.

In the video he says, "Hi, Michelle, I really want you to

come visit me. I really want to see you; let me show you my life." He showed me around his apartment, his cat; he took the camera on the bike with him and showed me his favorite bike path and bakery and some friends. When I tell you that I showed everyone this video around town, I did everything but submit this video to the Sundance Film Festival. I was so taken aback. It was the nicest, most romantic thing anyone has ever done for me. How could I not try to see this boy? I called one of my best friends since the ninth grade. My friend Rasheem, who's a handsome Black dude that did a little modeling. In my mind, I wasn't trying to start anything or make anyone jealous. Rasheem and I were planning a trip anyway, it had been a while. This was the perfect opportunity for one of my best male friends to tell me whether I was boy crazy or this guy was the real deal. Sometimes you need a friend to check you and see how you're doing. You can't be making all these decisions by yourself; you need to check in with someone who knows you best. That was Rasheem for me. Plus I needed to see how Gijs was gonna act with my friends. As a stand-up comic you have a lot of guy friends. It doesn't mean you wanna do anything with them; for the most part they're all babies. Sorry male comics, you know it's true.

Rasheem and I landed in Amsterdam. I ran to the bathroom and got the hot spots with a moist towelette a la Darcy in *90 Day Fiancé* getting ready to see Tom for the first time, minus the latex pants of course. I had on H&M stretch jeans and cowboy boots—ya girl is about that comfort huney!!! When we finally got through customs and went out to meet Gijs he welcomed us with open arms. He gave me the warmest kiss. And he hugged Rasheem immediately and said welcome to Amsterdam, brother. That was the sweetest way he could've greeted him. The good thing about talking to someone so far away, I'd been able to act like the person I wanted to be. The best version of myself. Cool, calm, chill, collected, all that shit. Who knows if I'd be able to keep this up, but so far it was working.

The week ended up being so damn magical. Gijs couldn't be more of a gentleman. He'd open doors, get rounds at bars. His apartment was just as cute as it was on the video. He was a great tour guide. Rasheem and I rented bikes so we could get around town with him, and I'm sorry, but attractive Black people on bikes in Europe is the closest you'll ever get to seeing Santa or touching a rainbow. The whole trip worked out perfectly. It was the week of my birthday, and I know that's a lot of pressure for a dude. Going with Rasheem was also great, because if anyone asked why I was going to Amsterdam I didn't have to say, "To see if love is real." I'd say, "Rasheem and I haven't been out of the country in a while." I had a Jamaican cousin who lived ten minutes away by bike from Gijs. I had no idea she was so close and that Amsterdam was so small. My cousin Marie was truly a godsend in Amsterdam. It's already a beautiful place, but to have family there that can show you where the Black folks go to have good food and dance was next level. Because my cousin Marie is gay, she couldn't stay in Jamaica, it was too dangerous. I can't believe she ended up in Amsterdam just minutes down the street from my new friend that's a boy who's not officially a boyfriend!

We all hung tough. We went to cafés, bars, saw a coffee shop. A coffee shop in the Netherlands is where you can buy a joint or an edible. Whatever your little touristy heart desires. They don't serve alcohol at these places, which is why it's called a coffee shop! You can have tea and your joint! Or you can have an edible in your tea!

Gijs took me to a really cute old colonial place outside of Amsterdam for my birthday. It was so sweet. It was an old town where fishermen would go to buy and sell eel. Then Gijs took me to a place that had old-timey photos. I don't know how this guy knew that was the perfect birthday present. I had never done an old-timey photo, and by far that is my most favorite picture of us.

What I loved about him is that it felt easy. We were compatible but not so much alike that we could get easily bored. He had really sweet gestures to show me that he liked me and was into me that weren't your regular run-of-the-mill. Like making the video, putting the time in on the phone when most guys give you that "I don't do the phone" bullshit. Even taking me to an old village to take a picture is making memories—not just taking me to a nice restaurant that everyone else would go to. Helping me lock up my bike since I was

Gijs and I dressed up in traditional Dutch garb at this fun studio in Volendam. I look like a Puerto Rican milkmaid, and I'm here for it!
Photo by Foto de Boer, Photoshop Volendam Haven 82 Volendam

in another country. Being kind to my friend and making sure he didn't feel like a third wheel. I loved all this shit.

What I needed help with was wrapping my mind around my jealous, petty ass when I would drink. These Dutch women were tough to read. And call me crazy, but this is what I recognized right off the bat: Dutch men have more female yin energy. They're worried about everyone else and sensitive. Dutch women are hard. Not hard like an old Russian lady who's been through some shit, smoking four packs of cigarettes a day. No, not that hard. I'm talking hard like, they don't laugh with strangers easily (I'm the stranger). So here I am, in the middle of an Amsterdam trip with my lovely guy that I'm falling for, and my boy. And meeting his friends after lots of day drinking 'cause, hey, it's vacation and I'm thirty years old about to turn thirty-one, thirty fun!! Everyone speaks English in Holland—that's a fact. But for some reason, when I would meet Gijs' girlfriends, they would just speak Dutch to him. That annoyed the shit out of me.

Gijs also smoked cigarettes; I did not. I actually had never dated a smoker. It was new for me. When Gijs would go smoke, he'd leave me and go outside for a good thirty to forty-five minutes. I felt so abandoned. I know that sounds crazy, but I didn't know anything else to compare it to. It sounds stupid, I know, but at the time I didn't understand the culture of smoking. You drunkenly meet people outside of wherever you are, and to me that sounded like too much. My second night there the real Buteau came out. Rasheem ended up hanging with this dope Amsterdam chick, plus he wasn't into drinking, so I was riding solo.

The longer Gijs stayed outside laughing and smoking, the madder I got. I would watch him from a small window from the back of the club like I was staking out a suspect or a Jamaican mom cleaning her 5th grader's bedroom. I saw him throw his head back, laughing at a joke, and I got even MORE MAD. Then I saw him go for another cigarette from some young chick's box. He lit his cigarette, then lit hers, and I saw red. I saw black. I saw stripes like I was in *Beetlejuice*. That was it, I'm not gonna be disrespected like this! I marched out there and looked at him and said, "Really, muthafucka?" and just walked away. I didn't know where I was going. I didn't know where he lived. I didn't know how to speak Dutch. I didn't see any taxis or buses. I was a hot mess with no plan but lots of attitude.

He caught up to me, and we had it out. I told him I didn't like that he left me. He didn't think he left me. This is the thing about the beginning of a relationship: You have to fight. You have to raise your voice and figure shit out. Don't get me wrong, this can't be your whole relationship, but you do have to stand your ground. If you're not comfortable with something you have to speak up. You can't assume that'll be just the one time, or that you'll become comfortable with it. So we're having our first argument, and it was a drunken argument. I can't even tell you all what was said 'cause the beer in Holland has a higher alcohol content, but we both got our point across and walked home silently. The next morning I was embarrassed for walking off and making a scene (by Dutch standards, not by Jersey food court mall standards). Though shit, that was nothing for a Jersey girl—that was me being a lady. Walking the fuck off and not breaking anything. We were both sorry for getting mad, which was dope. He didn't realize how I felt waiting for him, and I didn't realize he was someone I could finally trust.

At the end of the week it felt like we had been together for a month, in a good way. We laughed, I cried, we fought, I cried, we had a great time, yeah, you guessed it, she cried! I had to leave soon, I didn't want to, my whole body was numb. The night before I left we were at his favorite bar. We both didn't want me to go. It was sad, and also amazing in that it confirmed everything we were feeling for each other. I asked him, do you love me? He just looked at me like he didn't understand these words together in a sentence. Like I just asked him the toughest question on *Who Wants to Be a Millionaire.*

"Do you love me?"

"Um, I have um, feelings of love toward you."

"What the fuck does that mean?"

"That it is possible soon."

"What the fuck does that mean?"

"That it is there."

"What the fuck is where? I'm not going to go home without you telling me you love me."

"The feelings are, you know, um, there."

"Well, if they're there. Say it."

"You want me to say it?"

"YES." (Eye roll)

"Are you making me say it?"

"YES." (More eye rolling.)

"Oh, shit. Okay, um. Well, uh, Michelle, I do have the feelings. I, okay, I love you."

"You what?" (Smiling, lady boner growing.)

"I love you."

"I love you, too, babe, awww."

That's a real love story, y'all. I made him tell me he loved me. I'm not gonna wait for him to figure it out. Fuck that shit. I'm gonna help him along the way. I knew who I wanted to spend my time with. I wouldn't want to argue and fight with anyone else. I didn't even know what love languages were back then, but he was definitely speaking mine.

SURVIVING HOLLAND

When we started dating and he'd visit America it was always a thaaaang when he introduced himself. The Dutch pronunciation of the *G* doesn't exist in the American alphabet, so every time he meets a friend here goes this mini Rosetta Stone Dutch lesson. Sort of like your Indian friend growing up who had a traditional name that everyone botched until she changed her name to Lisa. I don't think Americans are used to white people having exotic names they can't pronounce. The Dutch *G* is like the sound of a TV that has static on. Or if you don't remember that, the lowest setting on a white noise machine. So . . . Gijs = Hhhhhh + *ice*. And when Gijs introduces himself to people it always goes like this:

"Hi, I'm Gijs."

"Sorry?"

"Gijs."

"Kite?"

"It's Dutch . . ."

"Spell it?"

"G. I. J. S."

"Oh, shit, how do you say that?"

"Gijs."

"Do you have a nickname?"

My mother is from Jamaica and sounds like a singsongy leprechaun. When I told her his name I tried to keep it simple and pronounce it like Hice, but in hindsight, telling her his name began with an H was a mistake. In Jamaica, when you have a word that begins with the letter *H*, you don't pronounce the *H*. Instead of *hello*, you say *'ello*. So my mother and the rest of my Jamaican family calls him Ice. Like the white rapper from the nineties who's down with the Insane Clown Posse but can't make good decisions. My Haitian father says *Gijs* like he's got French Tourette's. As if saying his name wrong a few times in a row will somehow make it sound right? He'll say *rice* three times in a row like it's a tick. It's so embarrassing. It's mortifying, really. I'd be happier if he just called him Son or Dutchie or even My Man (in his seventies-disco-Afro voice).

When Gijs would visit me in New York, he realized that he needed to have a restaurant reservation under an alias because I could have cooked us a nine-course dinner by the time he finished his Gijs-tory. One time he called to make a rezzy under the name Bob. I actually heard him say "Yeah, that's spelled *B-O-B*." Kind of not necessary considering that's the name of every one of my friend's dads. Also, I wouldn't ever have sex with someone named Bob for that very reason. His restaurant name is James now. James Jameson to be exact; I live and I die.

We dated long-distance for almost two years, and he always made an effort to let me know he was thinking of a bitch. Every day I would wake up to an email with the subject "Song of the Day." There was a lot of Roy Ayers "Love Will Bring Us Back Together" and "Everybody Loves the Sunshine"—real panty-dropping-type shit. He also came up with this other really cute idea for when I was on a plane and he was home. I'd get Wi-Fi on the plane to text him, and we'd pick a movie and watch it at the same time. We could still be doing something together despite being apart. That boy good. (One more reason to spread.)

We had a lot in common, but it was our differences that kept me most intrigued. I believe Dutch people are born on their bikes and they literally ride out of their mothers' vaginas. Which might explain why Dutch moms don't smile very much. On my third visit to Amsterdam, Gijs bought me my own bike so I would have transportation. (Lots of stretching for all the spreading.) He rode like Lance Armstrong and I'd go so slow it looked like I was on a stationary bike. Tiny European cobblestone hills and massive American titties do not mix. I looked like the person who has never been to Soul Cycle and five minutes into the class was like, "What did I get myself into?"

One time it was snowing, and he still insisted we ride our bikes to the bar. I'm from New York City, bitch! We take a cab two blocks when it snows! I have zero desire to be outside in the snow at all, let alone becoming one with it on my bike. I mean, what the what? I felt like that one female survivor in *Alive*. My eyeliner ran all over my face, in my eyes, in my nose, and I started to cry. I wiped my makeup off with my scarf and showed up to the bar makeup-free, like I had just lived through a literal cold war. I felt very Dutch.

People in Holland also hop on and off the back of one another's bikes like frogs on lily pads. It's the weirdest shit I've ever seen. The bike is in motion, then you run a little bit, and hop on the back. In front of people. Running and hopping and in public. Who does that? They all look like lanky blond Ninja Warriors playing leapfrog and risking sterility. After watching *Kiss the Girls* I thought being stalked, kidnapped, and turned into a sex slave waiting for Morgan Freeman to rescue me would be my worst nightmare, but no. It was this bike-hopping bullshit. When I got on the back of Gijs's bike for the first time, he was soooo very polite and pretended it was super easy having my then-size-16 lady bits in tow—but it was a struggle 'cause: gravity? He looked like a tugboat towing a sassy cruise ship.

After months of hard work and communication, I finally nailed the pronunciation of my Dutchie's name. Then I had to meet all his friends and family. His friends are named Thijs, Jan Anne, Marjolijen, Edo, Manon, Cees, Jelle, Martijn, Tjeerd, Tuen, and Bregie. They're all really tall, very handsome artists who kiss one another on the lips, sit on one another's laps, and come up with small-business plans at the dinner table that their government will most likely fund just 'cause.

Gijs was so sweet and great, but come on. Long-distance with a seemingly perfect guy? I was so sure he'd cheat on me; it'd be so easy. I tried to look through his phone a couple of times, but everyone's name was so weird I didn't know if they were male or female. He didn't even give me a reason to look through his phone, it was just my go-to because I was so used to being hurt. The distance was so long and the feelings were so strong, I just had to trust him with my heart. But if we're being totally honest, I was waiting for the other wooden shoe to drop.

Entering a new relationship that's good for you after a string of terrible ones is a mind fuck. You don't mean to bring that caged-animal energy to the table, but it sho' do pop up. Like that zit in the crease of your nose after a long flight? The only way I could get through trusting him, and not seeming like a crazy person checking his phone, was faking it till I made it. I hate lies. I hate fake. But I truly just pretended to be the best version of myself. I forced a smile on my face every time I was in an awkward situation—and not to be that person, but it worked. Dutch people were all, *She's always in such a good mood, she's so chill, she's down for anything!* (They said that shit in Dutch though). Rosetta Stone come through for ya girl, bitch!

CELEBRATING HANNEKE

When I first met his mom, Hanneke, she was so excited to see me it was overwhelming. She looked like one of those people who just got their name called for *The Price Is Right*. She was running in circles around me, blowing cigarette smoke in my face. She was obsessed with my face. Like she just saw her favorite celebrity at Madame Tussauds and couldn't believe how lifelike it was. And yes, her name sounds like Hanukkah but she insists it doesn't. It totally does. My first visit to her house, she showed me Gijs's Christmas list from when he was eleven:

- Skateboard
- Stickers for my skateboard
- Tropical girlfriend
- Cash

It was adorable. Then she said, "I'd always knew he would marry a negro!!!"

THE GIFT HORSE

The first time I met his sister, I wanted to bring her a gift. She lives on a horse farm where she raises horses, so when I found this sixty-euro horse-head candle, I thought it was perfs. I mean, she loves horses, and what woman doesn't love a good candle? The horse head was heavy, so, so heavy. When it was in the bag it felt like I was carrying a real horse head. When I hopped on my bike to follow Gijs back to his apartment, I felt super Dutch because this was the first time I was riding my bike with a heavy bag on the handlebars, which is super common there. We rode over some grooves in the street for the tram cars and my tire got caught. My bike stood still for one short terrifying second and then tilted over like the *Titanic*. I went down, hard. I didn't want to break the horse head. I didn't want my dress to blow up. I didn't want to hit my face on the pavement. All of that happened anyway. I pulled myself up and realized that I just ate shit with an overpriced horse-head candle in front of a full patio bar of Dutch people. Then I realized there was a tram behind me full of Dutch people who weren't like, *Is she okay?* They were like, *Get the fuck up, you dummy! Why do you have a horse head in a plastic bag? That looks terrifying. And why are you wearing men's cowboy boots with that dress? You're not Six from* Blossom. Gijs, who was in the distance riding his bike in a small circle, asked/yelled if I was okay. Physically? Sort of. Emotionally? Ruined. By the time I got this dumb candle to his sister, I'm not sure she knew what to make of it. The horse was missing a piece of its nose, but she said that's what made it special. When I was leaving her place, she confessed she wasn't sure if she could look at a melted horse face, so she might not light it. I told her I understood. It was her journey now.

OMA

The only person that doesn't speak English is his ninety-six-year-old grandma, and I wished I could converse with her. She looks like a happier Queen of England. Because my name is Michelle, Oma speaks French to me, even though I never answer her or have any idea what she's saying. Apparently she likes to tell me stories of how she enjoyed very dark rum when she would visit the Caribbean. She always throws a little wink in there when she says it, so I don't know if she's talking about dark rum or hooking up with a Black guy. I'll stick with curtain #2, Wayne. Oma is always dressed to the nines and hasn't worn a bathing suit since Hoover was president. She has three Pomeranians that sit on her lap at all times. These lap dogs are called "pussy lickers" in Holland. TruTV! When I heard her say something in Dutch about holding her pussy licker, I almost fell out of my seat. The Dutch word for it is *kuttenlikkertje.*

SKIING

Gijs has always wanted me to go skiing with him, but I just cannot. When he first told me, "I've been skiing in the Alps since I was two," all I heard was, "I have a very good inheritance coming to me . . ." Like I've said, my parents are from Jamaica and Haiti. Our family vacation consisted of going to the beach wearing shower caps followed by a fish fry. Sports we grew up with in Jamaica are running down the street with an old tire, or figuring out if your cousin is really your sibling out of wedlock. The only time our family would be going up and down a mountain is if we were climbing Dunn's River Falls in Ocho Rios. I am so far removed from skiing that when Gijs decided to take me for the first time last February I thought we were celebrating Black History Month. He's like, "It's Valentine's Day, *liefie.*" Whoopsie. I knew skiing was expensive but not open-another-credit-card expensive. I spent so much money trying to look like a Black Lindsey Vonn that

I didn't have any money left to actually get a lift ticket. I decided to get a lesson. I wanted to get as good as one of the seven-year-old Aryan poster children named Taylor or Forest on the bunny slope. Why is every rich kid named Taylor or Forest? Just, bye.

As if I wasn't nervous enough, my ski instructor looked like he'd need a good seventy-two hours before he could pass a drug test. The first thing he said to me was "We met for a reason; either you're a lesson or a blessing." I was like, *Look, Oprah, I enjoy a joint once in a while, too, but this is for serious. I have an HMO, not a PPO. I need to learn how to fucking stop, because this pizza/french fry/nacho shit isn't working.*

He said calmly, "Don't listen to what your body wants to do, listen to what I tell you to do with your body." Apparently my body wasn't a good listener. I fell so many times I'm celebrating next Valentine's Day with a hip replacement. I decided to skip the double-black diamonds and do some double-Black-Label shots in the lodge. Want a doable winter sport? Try sitting next to a fireplace, drinking booze, and making bets on how long these rich couples will stay married. The only skiing I'll be doing again is watching water skiing. I'll be sitting on a beach in my plus-size tankini getting my hair braided by someone who looks like my cousin. Girl, bye.

SAY YES TO THE STRESS

THE ENGAGEMENT

When Gijs proposed to me I was honestly floored. Completely taken aback. Frankly, I was still struggling to pronounce his name, and we couldn't afford our relationship. We had been going strong for almost a year and a half, long-distance. We had no damn money, but we had miles, coupons, and faith in our bond. I sublet my apartment to buy a flight to see him. He sold his 1979 Mercedes 450SEL to come visit me. By any means possible, we were making this little relationship grow. I had planned on spending the summer in Amsterdam with him. I thought, okay—three months with someone is the longest that I would have lived with a boy, and my hope would be that we still liked each other at the end of the summer. Who knew? It was so much more than that.

We took our first vacation together to the south of Spain for a long weekend. It was amazing. It was warm, the people were friendly, and the drinks were cheap. I went topless on the beach for like five minutes. It would've been longer, but there were lots of construction workers. With my *National Geographic* titties, I wasn't about to give them a free show.

Gijs rented a moped scooter to cart us around, and I remember hugging him harder than any man I've ever been with. Not just because I loved him but also because I was scared shitless. We scooted around Costa Blanca, Spain, like we were in *Ocean's 8* or some shit. I really wanted to be cool with being on a bike, but I am so uncool when it comes to any semi-dangerous situation that involves speed. Meanwhile Bear Grylls over here wanted to take a ride up a mountain at night, sail a boat with just the two of us on the Mediterranean, and go deep-sea fishing. What in the actual fuck? I know I've never presented myself as Kate Hudson in every movie and Fabletics commercial, so why were we there doing all that? Then our last night there homeboy proposes. Now, I don't know what Don Draper–type muthafucker tells women they need a diamond to be engaged, but that's some bullshit. I'm not into jewelry anyway, and sorry to kill your joy, honeys, but I don't need to wonder if some poor African kid got his hand cut off so I can have a nice rock.

What he gave me was so special. It was three stones. An imperfect pearl, an amethyst, and a crystal. Oh man, he was so cute and emotional. He sounded like he had rom-com Tourette's. We were on the beach at night, at the foot of a mountain, and there he went: "I love you, you had me at hello, you complete me."

I'm like, "You okay? Do you smell burning toast?"

He said, "I'm trying to marry you!"

It was so sweet. I said yes! DUH.

We hopped on our Fisher-Price scooter to celebrate. We went into some bar that looked cool. Immediately the waitress put down aioli and bread. Oh cute, we thought—this place is dope. We had a beer and asked for the check. When we got the check the aioli was on it, and it was fifteen dollars. Who the fuck is out here payin' fifteen dollars for some mayonnaise with garlic? Get the fuck outta here with all that. We told the waitress we didn't know you had to pay for it. Here she goes, starting to complain in Spanish to her manager. He comes over and just straight-up starts yelling at us, like he's our gym teacher. Gijs told him, "It was on the table! No one told us! ¡No gracias! We are leaving!" Yaaas, honey! That is my man, bitches! Back up! I was so proud of him and turned on. Justice was served!!!

As we were about to hop on our bike after high-fiving over how cool we are, we realized, both at the same moment—shit. We left our helmets inside at the table. Oh fuck. We held our heads up high and walked back into that dumb bar like we were Shangela coming back to *RuPaul's Drag Race* for redemption. We walked in, avoided eye contact, picked up our helmets, and sashayed away. If I had known the road that lay ahead, I wish we had just scooted right into a chapel and locked it down that night.

THE WEDDING

If you ever find yourself dreaming of what your wedding day will be like, keep in mind that nightmares exist. Those nightmares come in the form of everyone who wants your wedding day to be theirs. I was over the moon to tell my family that we were engaged. The minute I told my mom she squealed, "We're getting married!" Yes, you heard right. Which meant after the hugs and kisses and congratulations, there were going to be a lot of rules to be followed. As an only child, the obligation I had to make my parents happy was so in my face I couldn't see around it. Add the fact that my uncle is an archbishop in Jamaica? Throw in some standard run-of-the-mill Catholic guilt with a pinch of "Your boyfriend wasn't baptized?" You've got a recipe for a Costco-size therapy session.

Gijs had to get a crash course in Caribbean Catholicism and trust, playing the tambourine at mass is all fun and good—until we're dealing with an actual sacrament. See, your typical Dutch weddings are small. They take place in a restaurant or tricked-out farm instead of a church. They're also cheap, which could be a good thing if you think about it. You don't have to impress anyone, or do anything over-the-top. It's like going to school wearing a uniform. It's happening, but nobody's paying too much attention. American Caribbean weddings are an inch away from a Miss Universe beauty pageant. Caribbean people testifying to church music, then one hour later clapping their booties to dancehall music.

Everything had to be just right, and there wasn't anyone who didn't have something to say.

When I showed my mother my dress, a lovely ethereal Grecian goddess off-the-shoulder number, I believe her words were, "Ah dun' know." Even my friends were all over me "to make better decisions." They were either super traditional—"Remember, something old, something new, something borrowed, and something blue!"—or completely against the grain: "Fuck that! Why do you even have to wear a dress?!" Nobody cared what Gijs and I wanted.

I thought I'd have a barefoot-on-the-beach, white-tea-votive, ten-apple-pie–type wedding. Instead, I had an overly religious, superhot-and-humid-Fort-Lauderdale-in-the-middle-of-hurricane-season, baby-crying-the-entire-time-I-was-reading-my-vows (yeah, it's on tape, FYI), judgy-and-miserable, Dutch-people-dripping-like-Yankee-Candles-they're-so-hot–type wedding. To make matters worse, Gijs had never been to an American wedding before. I had to explain every step to him, down to a wedding dance. "Why do we need caterers to serve guests food? Why do we need a cake? Why do we have to do a dance?" I told him that it's customary for the new couple to do a dance, and you married a bish who dances! He didn't want to, but I made him. We practiced and practiced and ya know what? No one cared. It was a huge fail. We danced to a song called "Word Love" by a lesser-known Rhianna (truly, this is another singer named Rihanna). I don't like to live in regret, but once a year we talk about our wedding and we're both in a state of why and what the fuck? It almost brings us closer? Like, we have survived some shit; we've overcome.

The most interesting part in all of this is that my mother and father had basically eloped on their lunch break. They were planning a wedding, but my mom was going to be deported from the United States last-minute, so they had to get it done. I couldn't help but wonder if my grandmother gave my mom as much shit as my mom was giving me. My parents were so happy, I couldn't find the words to speak up and ultimately feel like I was disappointing them.

During the reception the hits just kept coming. My Jamaican family kept requesting "Ice Ice Baby," but I was so over it. One of my friends was dating a dude that was a hypochondriac. He had earplugs the whole weekend, thought he was going to get sick, and complained that his tooth hurt. His orange earplugs looked very *Making a Murderer*. Since then, they've broken up. The room we had our reception in was the top circular room of the Hilton, which sounds amazing. But the room also slowly rotates, and people were so drunk and high they never knew where they were going. We constantly had to use the guy with the bright orange earplugs as a navigation landmark.

Men's Wearhouse got all the sizes wrong for Gijs's groomsmen, so they looked like they stepped out of a clown car. People came out last-minute wanting to do speeches, which ran way too long. It felt like a hot, sticky, dressed-up town hall. We got it, everyone, yes, thank you. We shut it down after Gijs's mom thanked everyone in my family for helping him with his green card—but not before giving a shout-out to the cat he had to give away back in Holland.

Making matters worse, I was literally light-headed the whole day. I dieted so hard for this wedding I dropped forty pounds. My expensive wedding dress was too big and kept falling off me. I had a couple bites of mashed potato and a tequila, and I damn near blacked out. It was too much; I did too much. So don't diet too hard before your wedding or any special occasion—you're perfect the way you are, and that's why that special person is ready to spend their life with you.

Everyone was clawing at us. We didn't have a moment to chill or relax without someone telling us a long-winded story about their wedding, or our decorations, or how happy they were for us, or how weird someone was acting toward them. Can we all stop treating brides and grooms like they're customer service at Target? They can't fix shit for you, and they're thinking about a million other things anyway. All you have to say to someone on their wedding day is, "Damn, this is great. Do you need a water?"

The first rule of weddings is who pays has the say. Since Gijs and I were broke artists, we didn't have much say. Look, I don't want to seem ungrateful, because my parents have worked hard for what they have. They've come from humble beginnings and made their way in America. That's amazing. I'm in awe of them. But (oh come on, you knew there was a but!) if I'm being totally honest, our wedding was for them, it wasn't for us. That's a life lesson for me—you can't force your plans on someone else. We don't have any pictures from our wedding up in our home. We've been married ten years, and like that quote on the magnet, "It's about the marriage, not the wedding." Gijs and I got lost in the sauce when it came to our wedding, but that made us stick even more to our own plans and who we are as a couple (another life lesson). I'm so gahtdamn glad that's what came out of it. I knew I was marrying the right man when we bounced out of that bar in Spain like two pimps.

TOOTH BE TOLD

In 2012 I moved to Los Angeles for two short years. Or maybe one long year . . . oh man, I don't actually remember. See, when you live in a place with no seasons it's like being in a vacuum. And the LA vacuum is the same every single damn day. It's beautiful out, you're trying a new diet, and somebody just asked you to read their screenplay. Rinse and repeat. In other places, you can pinpoint exactly what's going on just because of the weather: Fell down the stairs at Penn Station when it was snowing and broke my new glasses. Right. The winter from hell. The overwhelming memory I have during those two short years or one long one was that every aspiring actor had to have three things: a bright, shiny website; a bright, shiny way to pitch yourself to casting people; and bright, shiny white-ass teeth. Pearly ass, new-car-smell teef. Teeth so white they own a yacht in Nantucket. They wear salmon-colored pants and have ancestors that were directly involved with colonialism.

People are sooooo judgy about teeth. And it makes sense, I guess. Your grill is the most obvious reflection of what you think about yourself. We all have those ten we think we need to shed, or need to quit drinking wine around our in-laws on Thanksgiving, but that shit we can cover up or run away from. Teeth? They're right there on your face like a hygiene business card. They say "A woman can tell in thirty seconds whether she wants to sleep with a man." And it's all about the teeth. If a man has a bright, shiny, white smile we think, *Approachable. Responsible. Good job. Has power tools.*

Today there are so many affordable options to fix your teeth. You can order dental trays online, you can whiten them with ten-dollar gel from the drugstore, you can even layaway that shit! Back in the day you were fucked. You had to fly to the Dominican Republic or figure out how to smile without making it obvious that all your low self-esteem was stored in your mouth. I got pretty good at option number two because I couldn't afford option number one. For as long as I can remember I've always had teeth problems. People are always surprised, and I guess you wouldn't know it because DID YOU SEE THE COVER OF THIS BOOK?! I'm happy! I'm always smiling! Well, lemme tell ya, it wasn't always like that.

It's not that I had jacked teeth. But I had one jacked tooth. She was one gray bum tooth in the front of my damn face that stood out harder than Meghan Markle at a royal garden party. My shit was out there, just being lazy in the street holding up a sign "Will Work For Food." And what did I do about it? I put it on my to-do list.

I was always in and out of the dentist chair because I had cavities. I had sort of gotten used to the needle to numb the gums, the weird chalky-mint spit, and the rinse-your-mouth into a mini toilet bowl routine. But hands down, those X-rays are the worst. Can we not come up with a better system? It's like holding a pointy deck of cards in your mouth and waiting for someone to get a good selfie. And, oh, if that dental assistant doesn't get the picture right the first time? I'm leaving a bad review that takes longer to read than the emotion on Kim Kardashian's face. I knew general dental shit would always be a part of my life, but it took a true oral disaster for me to finally wake up about my bum tooth.

When I was editing overnights at WNBC my diet was way the fuck off. I was working from midnight to 9:30 a.m. for six years, and when your body is in morning mode you always feel hungover. It makes sense that you crave breakfast food. I was eating tons of bagels and doughnuts #carblife, and you know that saying you are what you eat? It's true. I was round, beige, and doughy. One time on the overnight shift I was editing with some random, fill-in substitute writer who looked like he should be upselling button-downs at Men's Express. As usual, I picked up a bagel. But not as usual, when I bit into it I heard a crunch. I thought, *Wow! This bagel is hard as fuck! It's not even an everything bagel and it's too early for day-olds.* When I pulled it out of my mouth and looked at it, a headline flashed before my eyes. "News Editor Becomes News After Finding Glass in Bagel." Then I felt my gums burning and freezing at the same time. Girl, I looked at the writer. He looked at me. We both looked at the bagel. Then he screamed. Then I screamed. Then he said, "Michelle! Your tooth is in the bagel!" I started to cry and just kept saying, "No, it's not," like some weird yoga chant. Then it just kind of turned into a very loud prayer because the fact of the matter is that I knew that my tooth was in this godforsaken bagel. It was truly an out-of-body experience, like fast and slow motion at the same time.

Do you remember in *Saving Private Ryan* when that bomb went off and blew out Tom Hanks's hearing and there was this like high-pitched frequency? That was me. This was the beginning of my personal way on my bum tooth. I had to work quickly and think fast because not only was I the editor, I was also the supervising editor. I was in charge of people. Adult people that were older than me and resented that I had been promoted so quickly. I always had something to prove. I had to run the video in and out of the edit rooms because that was my job. How the fuck was I going to get through work with a missing tooth? Right in the front, like Alfalfa! I even had the freckles!

The thing is, you never really know how many people you smile at in a day till your front fucking tooth goes missing in an Einstein's bagel. I didn't know what to do. I was maybe twenty-five or twenty-six. I did what I always do when

I don't know how to do something. I called my dad. Yep, self-proclaimed daddy's girl over here and, what, bitches? Shit, I know who my dad is, and in a big Caribbean family that's a big deal. So I lean on him. And honestly, I didn't know what the fuck he was gonna tell me. This wasn't a crisis that I had dealt with before, so it wasn't on my questions-for-the-rents list, which usually included "How often do I have to change the oil in the car?" or "What really is an APR?"

This was next level. What in the natural fuck happened to my face—it's a literal nightmare coming true. My father was very calming. Thank God, because it could've gone a lot of ways. He could've been like "I told you so!" But he wasn't like that at all. He was heartfelt and said in his Haitian accent, "That's okay, dawling, these things happen; you know this happened to me once, not at work, no one saw. So this is a lot worse. But it's okay. Save your tooth, don't throw it out, and go to the dentist first thing after you leave work."

This was a real John Quiñones what-would-you-do moment 'cause guess what? I threw that bagel out with my tooth in it. It was so sad to look at, I didn't know what to do! I guess I kinda thought, *Oh, I guess I'll just go to the tooth store and get a new one?* What the fuck? Before you go and judge me, ask yourself this: If your tooth came out in a bagel and you worked at a high-pressure job, and you were in your twenties and nothing similar had ever happened to you . . . what would *you* do? EXACTLY.

So here we are, people. This is why you write a book.

So folks know that you've lived. I don't know if this is more memoir or cautionary tale. A cry for help, perhaps. But oh, she has lived? You never know how your day is gonna go, right? You think, *It's just a Wednesday late night into Thursday morning shift!* Then you're on your knees in a dark edit bay going through the wet garbage trying to find the soggy bagel with your tooth in it. But nevertheless, you will find it. I found it; I'm done, right?

No, this is only the beginning.

My shift ended, but not without everyone on the sixth and seventh floor of 30 Rockefeller Center knowing what happened to my face. It was a slow news day, but not for my gums. And like I said, ya never really realize how many people you smile at until your front tooth has gone the fuck missing. This was just simply horrible.

As soon as work was over—that's right, I finished that overnight shift, 'cause I'm a *good-ass* manager—I went to my dentist, who thankfully was available. This was my first emergency appointment, ever. I knew that they existed, because it's an option when you call, but I had no idea that I would need it one day. The dentist was very kind and gentle. Now in hindsight, he was definitely overwhelmed and this was above his pay grade. He essentially broke down that I would need more work later, but for a quick fix, he had some really strong glue. He glued that shit together and it looked like a cracked tooth. But there it was, still the shape of a tooth. So I paid five hundred dollars and walked out of that office with no real fix.

Looking back at it, he was the used-car salesman of dentists. The glue worked for a few days until it didn't. I'd run back in there and he'd fix me up again. There goes another five hundred dollars. Again and again and so on. Just a little fix but I still had to come back for more.

My tooth became a conversation piece everywhere I went. I'd see people try not to stare at it as we were talking, but it was hard for them. I became wildly self-conscious. I wouldn't smile as big or laugh as loud. I'd purse my lips in a way that you couldn't see my teeth, which made me look even weirder, probably. When I laughed it looked like I was sucking on a lemon. I'd never had a huge issue with my body before. So this is #Adulting 101. Take. Care. Of. Yo. Shit. I really don't know what took me so long to take care of my tooth. It was always on the back burner even though I had the money to do it. I wasn't even afraid of the dentist. I don't know what my deal was. I probably looked like a hoarder making a to-do list to get to the piles of boxes and plastic bottles out of the kitchen to rediscover the countertop. "One day I'll get to it, what's the rush? We can use this mound of Macy's shopping bags for a table!"

For a little while I was known as the comic with the bad tooth. Not in huge circles but there was that one time I was onstage at a place called the Lantern. It was a cute little place in the West Village. My friend Eric Andre was in the back listening to my set. Then the mic hit my teeth gently, and that shit flew out like it was skydiving. MY FUCKING TOOTH

CAME OUT ON FUCKING STAGE. I quickly caught it, and said, "Gotta go, folks! Thanks!" Everyone in the audience that night—I mean, I don't know what the fuck they thought. Could you imagine going to a Sia concert and seeing her wig fall off and then we get to see her face? So glad that it was a free comedy show, because it's not like they can get their free back. In fact, that's their bad for going to a free show. What did they expect to see? Comics with dental insurance?

There were so many moments this cracked-ass tooth wouldn't stick. One time I went to the beach with my friends. It was all fun and games until a wave hit me too hard and I couldn't find my tooth in the water. Holy shit, was this the day I was gonna go home toothless? Turns out it was in my mouth and I almost swallowed it. What was I gonna do then? Shit my tooth out and stick it back in my mouth? Look, I'm not proud of this—but if we're not learning from our mistakes then what the fuck are we doing?

Another time I was on a date with this dude. He was the first self-proclaimed "foodie" I had met. This was before everyone was a walking Yelp review and was watching *Chopped*. I mean, shit, a "foodie" to me just meant that he had money to buy food. That's all it took for me. I'm a simple bitch and New York is pricey! He was cute, age-appropriate, spoke English perfectly (yeah, he was American, but that does not mean that he can speak English perfectly—duh, bish). We met at an overly trendy artisanal bar where the bartenders looked like they worked on the *Titanic*. This was the first time I had seen a bartender take thirty-seven minutes to peel a perfect orange for a seventeen-dollar old-fashioned like it was a circus trick.

That's when I was introduced to my first seafood tower. If you don't know what a seafood tower is, it's a *tower* of *seafood*. The waiter brought this LEGO situation of plates out, set it the fuck up, and then presented the most delicious fucking seafood you've ever seen. Proper crab legs, weird cut-up lobster bits that didn't even need melted butter, teeny-tiny shrimp salads that looked like they were from France, oysters that didn't look like a fetus. They were teeny-tiny bite-size silky yum-yums. I felt like a fat king at a wedding feast in *Game of Thrones*.

Usually a date with a dude would include a fried appetizer, splitting the bill, and him wearing a tracksuit despite not working out. But this dude was getting high-rise towers of crab without a *K*. If you have enough money to make me feel like I could get gout? I was having the time of my life. I felt like, wow, this is what my late twenties are about. Dating a dude that wanted to show me something, treat me like a woman. Then he made a little toast bite for me with this amazing tuna tartare. I put it in my mouth. I was so lost in the sauce and ready to dance in a trance with this *Bachelor*-season-two status that I forgot that I shouldn't be taking a direct bite of this toast situation because of my toof! I should've done the side bite.

As he put this crunchy-ass toast in my mouth, I took a

bite while gazing into his eyes. And BOOM. CRUNCH. FUCK! My tooth is caught up in sesame toast and tuna. I grabbed it and ran to the bathroom like I was escaping an asylum.

And so it goes. My first date in a five-star restaurant with someone who can actually afford it, and I've got a one-star tooth. I started to cry because I didn't know what to do. I came outside the bathroom with a partial tooth in hand. I told him I had a bad reaction to the tuna. I don't know what the fuck he thought. I'm sure he heard the noise: that scary, soul-sucking crack that had been haunting me since the bagel.

The date reminded me of when I was in college doing a presentation for my business advertising class and I dropped my index cards on the floor. As I reached to pick them up I was wearing my too-tight jeans. You know them too-tight jeans you wear 'cause all your other jeans are dirty. My pants ripped in front of the whole class, but I pretended that I farted instead, because somehow that would be less embarrassing?

Years went by with me thinking it was okay to have a half-assed tooth. I wasn't depressed, but I was definitely neglecting something important with my body. Why was I comfortable making do with nibbling sandwiches on the side of my mouth like some kinda big-tittied squirrel? That's not how adult life works.

In all my pictures I looked so sad. Every time I went out on a date I'd skip dinner and just go for a drink, claiming that I was cool like that and could do dinner by myself. Finally I just decided to fix it. Finding a dentist I could trust was hard. I would go to a few different dentists for second opinions and would be completely overwhelmed. I finally treated finding a good dentist like finding a good hairdresser: I asked a friend.

Even as an adult, Jersey Jen had still been going back to her childhood dentist and even her pediatrician.

I went to her dentist, and he couldn't have been kinder, more gentle, and honest. I was living in New York City, and even though his office in New Jersey was only eight miles away, I had to take a train to a bus to another bus and send a three-eyed raven to get to his office. He explained that I was just going to have to lose my tooth. Like, the whole thing had to come out because it was rotten. I asked him if I got this cavity because I would fall asleep in college without brushing my teeth. He laughed and said maybe. But the root of the problem—pun intended—is that bad teeth are hereditary. When he told me that, a rush of memories came flooding back to me about my parents and their dental mishaps.

I don't know why I had blocked out us being in Italy when I was fifteen. My mother, aunt, and I sat down to eat in a restaurant. While we were waiting for our food, my mom bit into a breadstick and her back tooth popped out. She cried, wrapped her tooth in her napkin, and then ate the homemade soft pasta for the rest of the trip. When we got home, she got it fixed and barely mentioned it again. She was gangsta about it.

I looked into the closest dentist to my New York City apartment that performed this tooth-implant surgery. There was a cosmetic dentist who could handle this business right across the street from my apartment. You mean to tell me a bish suffered all this time and there's a place right across the damn street? But it was just so, so, so expensive. And did you know that fixing your front tooth is considered by insurance to be cosmetic surgery? How the fuck is that even possible? My bad, aren't teeth a necessary part of your face? Teeth whitening, okay—cosmetic—but an actual tooth? A mandate!

So I did what any good American would do: I opened a credit card to pay for this surgery. The process was going to be a long and intense one. I'd have to do three rounds of surgery to remove the tooth, the root, everything. I'd have to let my gum knit together and heal for a few months before I got the implant installed. This meant I'd have to wear a flipper. *Cómo* say what? Yes, a flipper is a tooth attached to a retainer. You stick it in your mouth and sometimes use denture cream on it so it'll adhere to yo mouth and it doesn't fall the fuck out. *Real* hot.

I decided to do my big surgery while my mother was visiting so she could help me warm up that chicken broth. It was also around my twenty-eighth birthday, and comedy roasts were a thang.

A bunch of my comedian friends put together a birthday comedy roast for me, and it was truly one of the best, most memorable nights of my life. I was completely nervous about getting roasted though. You sit onstage, listening to jokes about you written by the people that know you the best—it's pretty insane. Even though my mom was in town, I asked her not to come. Instead we had a nice dinner together, where I had lots of wine, and headed to the roast.

Most of the comics in my life were there, and the jokes were fucking rolling. Rebecca Donohue hosted, Rasheem did some jokes about me, so did Jersey Jen. The comedy club owner came out, and he was dressed up as me. It was the highest compliment ever. Also, I think he just wanted to dress up like a girl? My friend Josh Filipowski paid homage to my old joke about tattoos: I've always said that if I get a tattoo I'll get one of a chicken wing on my face or a waterfall on my inner thigh. YOU GET IT—she sassy. Well, Josh showed up with a chicken wing drawn on his face.

I was pretty drunk when my friend Eric Andre came onstage and gave me a shot of warm brown tequila. I will never say anything racist except for when it comes to tequila. I like the white one better. Sorry, not sorry, das it. I can remember most of the day but that shot of tequila is when I sailed into a gray area toward a blackout abyss of *Look at me, I am the Captain now! / Jack, draw me like one of your French girls* realness. Eric killed, of course. From what I remember he called me the low-budget Lisa Bonet and called Rebecca the low-budget Shannen Doherty. At one point I tried to get up and roast everyone back, and that shit did not work. Ever see a little baby that just learned how to talk? That was me, just pure gibberish as I held the mic. I tried my best during the show to write notes, but if you looked at my notepad, it was just complete squiggly lines. Clean up on aisle five, we got a hot mess!! Apparently there was a big-ass cake at the end and people sang "Happy Birthday" to me? Too bad I was dancing to no music in my chair, spinning around like I was on the Mad Tea Party ride at Disneyland.

Apparently (which is the word I most often use while describing this night) there was an after-party at the bar downstairs. At that point I was like a sassy *Weekend at Bernie's*. (Sorry if you're a Gen Z—you'll just have to google all my old-ass references or ask your coolest aunt.) I was essentially toted around like a big-titty rag doll. Look, I'm not proud, but I've got to stand in my truth! I don't remember much except going to the bathroom and vomiting like I was in a movie about expelling a demon. I was hugging the toilet (learned my lesson about the bathtub), and my face looked like I just ran a half-marathon. I was carted out to my friend Shelly's car and she drove me home with my other friend Kristin in the passenger seat. I was in the back with the spins. Kristin was checking in on me while Shelly kept asking Kristin if our friend Baron was into her. Kristin's all, "Bitch! Who cares if this dude is into you or not? Our friend is about to throw up in your car!" And she'd be right. Shelly had to pull over to the shoulder of the West Side Highway.

They dropped me off at my front door and basically

handed me to my mom like the scene in *The Color Purple* where Shug Avery arrives that rainy night at Mister and Celie's house. Instead of saying "You sho is ugly!" my mom screamed, "Where de tooooth gone nah?" Yep, that part—my friends dropped me off at my apartment looking like a big-tittied Alfalfa. TMIA, #toothmissinginaction! I lost my damn flipper tooth that I just paid $750 for. I remember waking up in the middle of the night to use the bathroom and my mother was just watching me, like, checking if I was okay. Like I needed an intervention. I was embarrassed but so thankful she was there with me.

Did I mention that the day after the comedy roast I was supposed to have a meeting in the late afternoon at Comedy Central for a show I just booked? It was a prank show about race relations. I definitely thought about going into the meeting without a tooth, like "Surprise! Here's a joke I'm pitching about a cute girl with a missing tooth." But who hasn't lost their temporary tooth before a big meeting? What a life lesson: when you have a big day in the morning, keep an eye on your teeth.

My friend Kristin went back to the West Side Highway before my meeting to see if she could perhaps find the dried pile of vomit with my flipper in it. I thought this was such a good idea at the time. But as I'm writing this shit right now I'm like, ewwww. Was I just gonna put that tooth in my mouth after it had been baked in my vomit on a busy New York City street? I called the after-party pub that I got sick in to see if they found anything; that was an actual phone call I made. And what did they say about me after? This dumb bitch didn't call for her lost debit card, she wanted to see if there was a retainer with a fake tooth on it from two days ago. Oh man, this is a good time to apologize to all who were involved during this turbulent time. I ended up borrowing two hundred dollars from my mother, made sure I had some credit left on a card, and got another flipper. The dentist, wow, how do I describe his look? He was disappointed, shocked, even a little judgy? He watched me walk back to his dental chair like I was a rejected *American Idol* contestant back for the third time in a row.

I kept tabs on my new flipper like it was one of those baby dolls they give to high school kids. I was busy enough not to really think about how sad it is to lose a prominent tooth at such a young age, which was good, but wow it was a lot of work not to lose this shit again. I couldn't be that girl.

I eventually got the dental implant. A hole was drilled into my gum, and a metal rod with a tooth attached was inserted. The color was a bit off, but I didn't care. I was *SO HAPPY* to finally have a tooth that wouldn't go anywhere. I still couldn't bite into a sandwich at first, but I did learn a party trick with chicken wings. I'd just put the whole wing in my mouth and pull out the bone. Please get yo life, because people can't get enough of this dumb trick. It's like that old-school party trick where you tie cherry stems with your tongue to show people you really mean business in the bedroom. I don't know who made that shit up, but okay. Wow, look at the way that guy almost chokes on that cherry stem but then actually doesn't and somehow makes it into a little knot. He could really go to town on me 'cause he knows how to handle fruit stems. But what if I'm allergic to cherries?

When I eventually met my husband and got married, we moved to Los Angeles for those two short years/one long year/what is time or space? My smile was warm and sincere, but my teeth didn't measure up to everyone else's. All the actors I'd run into at acting class or at auditions had their teeth done. In my mind, I thought, if anything, as an actor you can just look like a person, because you'll be playing real people? Not newscasters or reality stars? However everyone had pearly whites, and that was one of the many things about living in Los Angeles that made me self-conscious.

One summer (or winter, LOL) my father-in-law visited from Holland. He's a dentist and heard me complain about my tooth at the dinner table. He said that he could help me fix my tooth, if I was interested. I said I'd love to, but I didn't know how I could afford that. He said he'd do it for free. I almost jumped for joy, like Steve Harvey just showed up to my door with a bunch of balloons for Publishers Clearing House. If I were to write a rom-com, this would be the climax. How amazing. How wonderful! I felt so seen, so validated, so heard. I couldn't have written a better happy ending. LOL . . . happy ending.

Talk about fucking your way to the right one. Who

cares about a diamond? I can't wear it as a tooth because I'm not as cool as Cardi B. The minute he said he'd do it for free. A new tooth! I knew it was gonna look good.

Gijs and I planned to go to Holland for the month of December. We were going to go for Christmas anyway, and since the tooth-fitting process takes a while, then why not go for the whole month? His father was about to retire, and this was his last hurrah. Did I mention I was excited though?! I didn't have to go to the Ukraine to get a new tooth!

The first appointment with Dr. Father-in-Law was pretty dope. He's clean and thorough and had sketches of what he wanted to do. His office was pristine as a kill room. His sister was his assistant, and it was so cute that this was a family affair. Less cute was that this was the first time I met her aaaaand she'd be seeing me toothless during the process, but whatever. She was sweet and kind and didn't speak much English, but she told me she loved Whitney Houston. Cool, cool. I'm glad she didn't ask me if I knew her. I felt like it was coming, and I didn't wanna have to break it to her. Ever tell a kid there's no Santa? This is exactly the same. So how does a big-titty bitch from Jersey end up in a dentist chair in Eindhoven, the Netherlands, getting a free custom-made tooth? This was my reparations moment! Light a candle! Gijs held my hand the whole time and was amused that he had seen me toothless. This is what wedding vows were made for: "To have and to hold, teeth or no teeth . . ."

At the time Gijs's mom was remarried to an older Dutch

guy named Ruud (sounds like Rude), which is ironic because that's exactly what he was: rude. He had a certain rich-dude tone that I could recognize, even when he was speaking Dutch. It was unbridled entitlement. He was a Karen wrapped up in an Ebenezer Scrooge display. Things came to a head; Gijs's mom ended up getting divorced in between my dental appointments that month. Talk about end-of-the-year emotional renovations!!

Gijs's family was so happy that he was there for his mom. I was too, and so was he. Gijs said if it wasn't for Michelle's tooth we wouldn't be here. Now look at that shit. For ten years that tooth gave me so much drama—awkward dates, lost flippers, weird auditions, horrible smiles, and bad blow jobs. But without that busted tooth, we would never have been there for Hanneke when she needed us most. Damn, thank you, busted-ass front tooth. And a special shout-out to the hard-ass Einstein's bagel that started it all.

IVF

One year, my mother got me health insurance for Christmas. Then two months later I found out I had a benign brain tumor. I told her not to ever get me another present again. I first knew something was wrong when I wasn't getting my period, and I knew I wasn't pregnant. I bought a few home pregnancy tests and they were all negative. And why are they locked up like the expensive champagne at the liquor store? I went to the gynecologist and he said I had a high level of a hormone called prolactin. This meant I could either have a benign brain tumor or a cyst on my ovary. I thought, *Wow, some MORE Christmas present!* I considered myself to be healthy. There's always a freshman fifteen that I could lose, but I could walk up and down steps no problem, bend over and tie my shoes without gasping for air—you know, real regular-life shit to be grateful for. A brain tumor was the craziest thing you could ever tell me. Where am I? A *Grey's Anatomy* episode? Full disclosure—I've never seen an episode of *Grey's* in its entirety, but every time I'm in a hotel room, it'll be on. And inevitably it's always somehow the same damn episode of Dr. Mc Mac Dream Dream that ends with a Leon Bridges song? Please do not revoke my Black-girl card: I fully support TGIT on ABC! I've even tried to wear the white shirts, drink overpriced red wine, eat popcorn, and watch *Scandal*. But popcorn is a terrible snack because it single-handedly absorbs all the moisture out of your mouth, and there's no way I cannot get red wine all over my tits (or as I like to call them, my fleshy bib.) They truly just catch all the things.

When you get some medical news, people try to comfort you in the weirdest ways. They'll say shit like, "Hey, look, that's great! *Benign* is the word you want to hear when you have a tumor!" See now, I thought "You don't have a tumor" is what I really wanted to hear. The word *benign* just helps it sound like the lesser of two evils. Kind of like saying my Dutch in-laws aren't racist, they're "just prejudiced." Or it's not AIDS, it's "just HIV!"

It's amazing how much we don't know about our bodies until something goes wrong and we have to fix it. Much like a car. Now imagine if your car suddenly gained thirty-five pounds and had such intense mood swings that it constantly thought about wrapping itself around a tree. When you have a mass on your pituitary gland like I do, it makes your body think it's pregnant. Fun, right? All the negatives but with no registry at Babies R Us. And apparently, you'll know it's getting worse if your peripheral vision gets blurry and you start lactating. Milk. Out. Of. Yo. Breasts. Periods. Shown. For. Effect. Congratulations, Michelle! It is a tumor!!! (In Arnold Schwarzenegger's voice.)

Since this was all hormone-related, my doctor told me I had to find an endocrinologist. After I asked if he could please use that word in a sentence, he said, "Endocrinology is the study of medicine that relates to the endocrine system, which is the system that controls hormones. An endocrinologist will deal with diseases caused by problems with hormones." And I will deal with learning how to spell *endocrinology*. I don't even know how to spell *definitely* without assistance. *Gorgeous* is a hard one, too. If you're definitely gorgeous then I'm definitely fucked trying to writing that. So yay, *E-N-D-O-C-R-I-N-O-L-O-G-Y*. That's my world now. Where's the trophy?

My first appointment was with an Indian doctor who had more hair coming out of his ears than his head. He was so old, sort of like E.T. in a lab coat. His hands were so shaky that his son had to take notes for him while he was examining me. But I believe old Indian doctors know more than any other doctors in the world, because they've lived through shit. (I know, I probably shouldn't have posted that on Zocdoc). Anyway, the first time I saw the doctor he told me to check my breasts for milk. Not even a "How was your subway ride getting here?" We're just gonna get to it? Cool, cool. In front of them I unhooked my bra and let loose the flesh tsunami known as my titties, and I started to squeeze. He yelled in an Indian accent, "Harder! Like you've milk-ving a cow!" Like I'm what now? I have many looks. Some people think I can sing or they're convinced I do poetry. Milking a cow has never been my look. Does my face suggest an urban farm-to-table situation? The closest I've ever been to camping was eating sushi with my hands on the subway. No, thanks.

The doctor shuffled over to me and wrapped his shaky hands around my big beautiful brown titty like he was holding a Big Mac for the first time. Then he started to pull on it, so hard! Like he was waterskiing, my titty was the rope, and he was desperately trying to fight his way through the chop. His son was trying to type notes on what was happening, but I couldn't tell from his face if he was going to laugh, cry, sneeze, or all three!

He yelled, "Father, are you okay?"

Yeah, I think "Father" is better than "Okay," grasshopper. My pregnant-not-pregnant brain was flooded with so many different questions, like fast motion and slow motion at the same time: *Why does everything feel like a joke? Why does my life have to be different from everyone else's? What have I done wrong in life to end up here? And why did my Tuesday afternoon have to turn into DIY Bollywood porn?* This wasn't a *Grey's Anatomy* Coldplay "Fix You" moment. This was an Adam Sandler movie moment. Even Drew Barrymore would be like, *No, thanks, I'll pass.*

A couple of years have gone by, and I've got my levels down to normal. Like most thirtysomethings, I have my annual MRI and cow-milking appointment. Oh, you don't do this once a year? Good for you. The tumor hasn't grown, which is great. I'm taking medication to shrink it, and it's far too small for surgery. So the question I'm faced with now is, if your body thinks it's already pregnant, why not actually get pregnant? My husband and I were ready to have a baby, 'cause let's face it, we're too cute to stop here. Plus when you're in an interracial relationship, the first thing anyone ever says is, "Awww, your kids are going to be so cute." I don't see same-race couples getting these compliments. No one is ever like "Awww, that inbred thing is so in right now." So while it feels like reparations in a compliment form, I'll take that shit. Interracial relationships have been illegal and frowned upon for so long, I think everyone is just now getting on the same page. So "You'll have the best-looking babies" translated really is "I'm totally fine with your choice! I'm not one of the bad ones! I loved *Loving*!" So by popular demand, we have to keep this going. He's Dutch and I've got big hair and freckles. Just to make people happy, we're gonna be forced to have the cutest Cabbage Patch–Uniqlo–ethnically ambiguous baby there ever was.

Husband and I tried and tried, but no baby. I went to an infertility doctor almost as a joke. Being Jamaican and Haitian, I knew girls personally who got pregnant while salsa dancing to Marc Anthony or twerking to Beenie Man. The doctor explained that in vitro fertilization, IVF, would be my only option. I'd only heard about this on very adult shows like *20/20* and *The View*, and from Kandi Burruss on *The Real Housewives of Atlanta*, but never in real life. The doctor ran down my schedule and explained the simple process of everything they would do:

1. Pump me up with hormones like a Perdue chicken. I'd have to basically become a very emotional pin cushion.

2. Monitor me three times a week with sonograms and blood tests to make sure I wouldn't become Octomom. (What's that bish doing now? And remember when she tried to look like Angelina Jolie? Amazing she had all those lip injections when she got all them diapers to change!)

3. Get put under general anesthesia (I do love a good nap) so homeboy (doctor) can collect my eggs like it's Easter at the White House. Afterward I'll be bloated like I'm three months pregnant. Or, in my case, like an hour after Thanksgiving dinner.

4. My husband's polite Dutch sperm and my sassy Caribbean egg will get mixed in a petri dish. Then the doctor will put it back in me like some Easy-Bake oven. And ding! Out will pop twins and a contract for a hair-care line for mixed babies.

5. PS, none of this might work.

I learned how misogynistic health care is when we had to pay twenty thousand dollars out of pocket, even though I have to do it because of a preexisting condition. By the way, that preexisting condition is called "being a woman." To say IVF is a rigorous process is beyond an understatement, especially for a bitch who thinks self-care is showering after you take a shit. I don't get fillers, I barely take vitamins, my cabinet is full of facial scrubs I've gotten in gift bags. I'm a tough and strong Caribbean-American woman who was going to have a lil' Saturday afternoon nookie sesh with the husband and hey hay hi everyone, we have good news! But no. All of a sudden, I'm a science project.

Everything with IVF is about timing. You've got to take your progesterone shots in the morning. Progesterone is a steroid hormone that you absolutely need in order to stay pregnant. Doctors mix it with olive oil so you can inject it in your arms, thighs, or upper booty. All dark meat situations. The needle is huge and thick and it's more painful than watching people find love on *90 Day Fiancé* with someone twenty-seven years younger than them. You have to follow this shot with a blood thinner called Lovenox, which is small shot in your tummy. When your blood is thin you bruise easily, so your tummy ends up looking like Apollo Creed's face at the end of *Rocky II*. Every day you have to find a new place on your body to take a shot because the good ripe spots are bruised and tired. When someone gives you a hug you try to not scream, "Ouch, bitch!" 'Cause you also, like, need that hug. Another fun thing you have to take is progesterone suppositories three times a day. So if you're like me and you have three or four meetings in a day in different offices all over town, you have to make sure you bring enough suppositories for the rest of the class. Oh! And they have to be refrigerated. It's hard to be all incognegro when you're covered in bruises and carting around medicine in pouches. Cut to me going to a meeting and asking the assistant if I can throw my medicine in the fridge. Then cut to me daytime fingering myself in a bathroom of a casting office, trying to get my progesterone suppository up in me properly, washing my hands thoroughly ('cause ew, y'all), then shaking hands with executives. Basically I was one hair-blowing fan shy of Beyoncé's busy schedule. (In my mind! She booked and busy.)

The first week of hormone shots I drank too much and told my husband I wanted a divorce. Then I cried. Then I laughed about crying. Then I cried because I couldn't stop laughing. Then I wrote a poem and followed that up with seven full-on male push-ups. That was week one.

Week two the crying continued, and we adopted a dog because, well, my ovaries told me I really needed to take care of something and my plants weren't enough. Those feelings were real! That's totally normal, right? My husband asked me what kind of dog I wanted, and I just answered "A big one!!" He ended up adopting a Lab/mastiff mix known as a mastador. She was adorable. Also, side note, I should've Google imaged what a mastiff was. I believe it's the word *massive*, because huge. She's big and black and beautiful and won't stop growing. Which is why I call her Precious. She's the size of a pony, and all I do is pick up shit. Which is how I've taken my mind off fertility treatments.

When I leave my house in the morning I look like a Puerto Rican Dolores Claiborne. Sporting a men's denim overall, looking beat from all the bending I'd been doing picking up shit. So much shit, like a broken soft-serve machine. When Lola the dog AKA Precious shits in public people cross the street because they don't feel safe. When I'm walking Lola with my friends they watch her shit and shut down like a host in *Westworld*. But did I mention she's so cute?

Finally I reached the end of the first cycle.

Turns out I got pregnant! I thought, yeah, of course I'm knocked up! I was about nine weeks and SO excited. Finally it was all falling into place. I was working on *The Nightly Show with Larry Wilmore* on Comedy Central. Water had just been discovered on Mars, and Bill Nye the Science Guy was the guest. The producers' angle for me was "Why wasn't this trending?" And they handed me a couple of terrible lines to say because they think "talking heads" shows need a variety of opinions in order to keep things interesting. One of them was "If the water on Mars was Caitlyn Jenner's tears, perhaps people would be more interested." Because Caitlyn had just come out that week, the whole thing blew up and I got bullied for the whole week.

Internet bullying is really the worst. You feel helpless, and people say the worst, most vile shit. I received death threats, was labeled "fat," "not funny," "anti-American," "anti-science" and my favorite, that I would be lucky to be raped by Bill Cosby. When you receive a certain amount of death and rape threats, Viacom security steps in and starts investigating. I had stand-up shows booked and wasn't sure if people would come after me. I feared for my safety. When people made eye contact with me, I'd jump a little bit, scared for what they would say. I went in for my weekly sonogram and lost the baby. I'm very sure it was stress. So a big shout-out to the trolls who bully people—I hope it's worth it.

There's never a convenient time to get bad news. Especially when it pertains to your body when you've gotta make money moves like Cardi B's first record deal out the strip clerb. My doctor said I had to schedule a D&C and he wanted me to have it on a Wednesday because that's the "only day they do them." Apparently it's safer to have a procedure then to let them expel naturally. And while the procedure takes a toll on your body, it's really good for the hospital's billing. My head was all over the place. I didn't know I could be so sad over someone I'd never met, but I was. At the same time, the pressure was on to tape a pilot in Los Angeles 'cause this business don't stop for anyone. I asked what would happen if I went to LA, and the doctor said a natural miscarriage could happen anytime. On a plane, during my shoot, buying plus-size nonsense at Forever 21. If not, I'd still be okay to go in for my procedure. So I hopped on a plane to Los Angeles to shoot this damn pilot 'cause, let's be honest, how else can I pay for all of this? So I put on some lashes and a smile and I flew to LA. The whole time I was sitting there and thinking, *I feel dead inside, literally.*

I didn't want to let people know what I was going through. Nobody wants to be the Debbie Downer when "Yay! We're shooting a pilot!" What was I going to say anyway? "Oh, don't mind me, guys, that's just me hemorrhaging. No, no! Don't get up! I'll just scoop up my uterus, put it in my tote bag, and be on my way. . . . Oh, catering has Granny Smith apples with peanut butter? Sure, I'll have some. Thanks."

Sitting on set all day, small talk was hard. Really hard. Every move I made, I thought, *Is this it? Is it happening now?* I was hurting and scared. Going through something horrible is also like doing something amazing, like skydiving. You have this weird compulsion to tell everyone about it, otherwise it somehow doesn't count. At the same time, I didn't wanna get a ton of attention for something so terrible when nobody knew me. So I just sat there and smiled, listening to people on set talk about their crazy to-do lists after we wrap. Damn, they had no idea what my to-do list was.

I tried to confide in one person, my makeup girl, because they hear everything, right? She ended up turning it into an episode of *The Doctors*, recommending holistic kale soup recipes, Reiki treatments, and for her final segment, showing me pictures of her kids like that shit was gonna somehow bring mine back to life. So I just played happy clown 'cause that's how I know how to get through the day. I kiki'd with Wanda Sykes, who was producing the pilot and that took my mind off things for a time. Then I took a red-eye back to New York. On that Wednesday I had the procedure. I rested for two days, then hosted for Rosie O'Donnell at Gotham Comedy Club. Even though I was crushed, I decided this would not be my ending.

I dove right back into the IVF. I thought, *Aight, girl, it worked the first time. This is just a weird stress thing; I can do this. Let's get right back into it; don't be sad about this. Just don't stress over stupid bullshit.* I worked the road doing gigs, traveling with my needles, never getting used to stabbing myself in the thigh before I put on a happy face onstage or on television. I did, however, get numb to the checkups. That's the only way you can survive waking up at 6:00 a.m., spreading for a man, feet in stirrups for your sonogram. I honestly never thought I'd spread my legs so much and *not* get knocked up. I learned lots of how-to tips for going to the gyno three times a week.

First, don't ever wear a onesie. You'll be the creepy naked girl at the office. Plus, E.T. in a lab coat killed the open-titty concept for me. Second, try putting scented lotion on your feet; you don't know what kind of day they've had, and while they're down there, they can enjoy this vanilla bean scent from Victoria's Secret. Ask a million questions because this shit is expensive and they won't tell you anything. Over-ask, like you're that vegan at Applebee's.

I went the holistic route this time and got pregnant again. Of course I did; this is what I was meant to do! I was like a

Puerto Rican Gwen Paltrow: I was all chia seeds, acai berries, no caffeine, acupuncture, maca powder, hemp seeds, minus a turban, I just can never find one that fits. I did everything I was supposed to. As I was out to dinner with Husband's Dutch friends I felt a weird pain in my stomach. And I knew it couldn't have been the overpriced guacamole or shrimp ceviche. I went to the bathroom and had my second miscarriage. When you watch movies or TV shows, there's always this moment where a wife will quietly ask her husband, "Can I talk to you in the kitchen for a second?" That's what I had to do at the dinner table. There's nothing worse than both sad and awkward.

I was pretty worn out. I read a bunch of stuff online about how people usually have two miscarriages, and you should be okay with that. But no matter how many stories I read, no matter how many other women had gone through it, it didn't matter. I was very much alone in this. I never told my mom a lot of details about it because it would turn into me over-explaining every little thing I was going through, paying for, etc. Any time she'd hear about someone doing IVF she'd always fuck it up and call it an IOU. Any time she called, her first question was always, "How's your husband?" Um, who gives a fuck? He's fine. He can have a kid till he's ninety. In fact, men could probably be dead and their sperm would still work. What a cruel irony that Mother Nature favors the man. So does Father Time.

Okay, okay, move on! I didn't even wanna think twice

about it. It was like the end of a marathon; I just wanted to keep going. I didn't care how beat-up I was, as long as I was hitting the finish line. I went right back into IVF right away. I was like, *Ticktock bitches, 'cause now I'm thirty-nine. I know I look good 'cause Blackish Don't Crackish ABC Family Tuesdays at 9:00 p.m., but let's go and get this done. This baby we ain't even had yet has already cost us over forty thousand dollars, so they better be like a video ho or pro athlete right out the gate.*

The best is when I had to meet with the VIPs. Last summer I had to fly to LA for a meeting with Paul Feig. Theee Paul Feig, huney! *Bridesmaids, Spy, Ghostbusters, The Heat*?! OMG YA—I wanna be the brown-titty Melissa McCarthy complete with a plus-size clothing line, let's do this, Paul! Now Mr. Feig and his bow ties are very busy, I get it. He kept pushing our meeting off, which he is totally entitled to do. I can't be like, "Oh, hey, manager, can Paul get his shit together 'cause I've only brought enough progesterone suppositories for six days and half of them have melted." Nah, boo. That's not how life works. My husband had to FedEx my medication out to me on dry ice, because this is our *New Normal* by Ryan Murphy.

When I met with Paul and his team they couldn't have been nicer. There was another man and woman who looked super cool and smart, like straight out of a page of *Scandal* and they were on Olivia's team #itshandled. On the outside, I was pitching a sitcom about my Dutch husband and his super white family. On the inside I was screaming, *Hey, guys! I'm not doing so well! I'm super hormonal! I Tori-Spelling-ugly-cry every time a kid auditions on* America's Got Talent! *I can't sleep in my friend's house 'cause she has a cat and it smells like a zoo. I'm tired of stabbing myself, and I don't know where to throw away syringes at a friend's house!! Also!!! I've just fingered myself with progesterone in your bathroom and I had to change my pants because I gave myself my shot the wrong way and my thigh wouldn't stop bleeding!!!! Who knew veins were that bloody? Like, they're not exaggerating on* Grey's Anatomy!

Instead I told them about how I'm the only person of color in his family, and ain't that crazy? We left off like we do in every meeting: You're great! I'm great! This is great! We're all so great! The meeting honestly was . . . great. As I made my way to the airport straight from his office, I realized my job was now not only to pitch myself but also not to have a breakdown while I'm pitching myself. In the airport I fingered myself with the progesterone that is not covered by insurance and got back on a plane home to my dogs, husband, toilet, and therapist. In that order.

I got pregnant. Again. Thank you, Ancestry.com. I'm fierce; I'm strong; I can do this. This is what my body was made for. Even though I was sad about the other miscarriages, I always thought I had a chance. When I was about six weeks pregnant, I got a call from my manager. "Channing Tatum is producing a live version of *Magic Mike* in Vegas and they're looking for a dynamic host that owns her sexuality and keeps the party going." I mean, minus the benign brain tumor and failed IVF attempts, I'm a perfect mix of sexy and cute as fuck, which is a very hard combination. (It also just naturally sort of happens when you've got big tits and freckles.) I go in to meet with the creative team. They're showing me videos of half-naked men bumping and grinding on women, women losing their shit, and then all of a sudden I feel like I'm bleeding and not in a good way. Side note: Can I just say that the creative team for Channing is amazing? They're like overly sexy, sweet-as-can-be adult cheerleaders. They kept showing me videos of men doing the boom-boom Cirque du Soleil, and I'm just thinking, *Welp, I really hope my embryo isn't all over their white chair.*

I didn't get the job. I didn't have the baby. And every time I see Channing Tatum I'm reminded of miscarriages. I can't help but laugh out loud while writing this, because there are so many other things to think of when you see Channing. Also, who is named Channing?

I felt like I had been through the wringer. Like the end of every boxing movie, where the main guy might have won the fight but he's so disfigured he can't enjoy the win. I decided to take a few months off and get my head right. In hindsight, I should've gone to therapy, a support group, booked a personal trainer to motivate me to work on my body, but I didn't. I ate everything I couldn't eat, drank everything I couldn't drink before. I threw myself into work, flying all over the place and just gaining more and more weight. It was really hard hanging out with friends and keeping up with everyone's lives. And while I seemed to be all right, my tunnel vision was zooming in on what I wanted most. Couples who never wanted a baby were all of a sudden having a baby. Friends who were pregnant during my miscarriages were further along in their pregnancy or had the baby. When friends started making their social media all about their babies' faces, I had to unfollow. Their lives were a constant reminder of what I didn't have in mine. I couldn't handle it. How dare you flaunt how hard it is to be a mother in hashtags? #TIREDMOM. I don't have the luxury of flaunting how hard it is to get pregnant in hashtags: #miscarriage #healthinsurance #IVF4life.

My husband and I thought about selling our Brooklyn brownstone, buying a house a bit up north, and using the extra funds for surrogacy or adoption. My doctor persuaded me not to give up our slice of Brooklyn, as he was sure we could stay pregnant.

"But why don't you just adopt?" We heard it all the time. And we looked into adoption, and those agencies won't allow couples to move forward with their applications if they're trying to get pregnant. (I know, I had no idea either.) We realized our cheapest option would be to go into IVF again. Six months later, we dropped another ten thousand dollars. Back to three shots a day, sore arms, bruised stomach, crazy up-and-down everything, and trying not to cry when passing the baby aisle in Target. Here. We. Go. I had a great run.

At thirty-nine I harvested twenty eggs. Out of those twenty, seven survived. We had them tested for PGS (preimplantation genetic screening) to see if there were any abnormalities. I was approaching my birthday, and what better time to try to get pregnant than for your fortieth? My friends kept asking me what gift I wanted. I was like, "Your uterus." It was time to move on.

I did another transfer, and you guessed it. But I never imagined I'd hear "You're pregnant" and feel so sad about it. I couldn't enjoy it at all. I couldn't swim, ride a bike, have a drink, sushi, or overpriced French cheese. Nothing about this brought me joy. I had been down this road, and it wasn't fun. I didn't have it in me to push forward. I kept crying the whole time, sad over my previous losses, and preparing myself for a new one. I was truly all over the place. If there had been a camera on me, I was totally reality-show ready. *Real Housewives of Bed-Stuy*. My log line would be "The only time I make it rain is in Flint, Michigan . . ." PS, what in the hell are we doing about Flint, Michigan?!

At our seven-week sonogram there wasn't a heartbeat. My doctor was speechless. And for the first time through this whole thing, my husband wasn't. He spoke up for me and said, "Enough. She's done enough. She's tired and she needs to be happy again." Feeling deflated and beyond depressed and wondering why I was back here again, I FaceTimed my mother. I wept as I told her what happened and that I'm officially done trying. That Gijs and I are going to refinance our house to pay for surrogacy. She was crying as well and said, "I was waiting for this phone call. Please stop doing this to your body. Your father and I have taken money out of our retirement; don't refinance your house or anything. We'll help pay for a surrogate. Find an agency you trust and let's make our dreams come true."

I'll never forget those words. I felt free, sad, tired, relieved, happy, and finally comforted by the one woman whose love meant more to me than anyone's.

Then she asked, "The baby will look like us, right?"

Aaaaaand here we go.

SURROGACY

When I found myself coming down after miscarriage number four after a little over two years of failed IVF, I still had embryos banked, so I decided to head down the surrogacy route. It's an understatement to say it's the road less traveled. I didn't know anyone else who'd done it; no one handed me a copy of the book *What to Expect When Someone Else Is Expecting Your Baby*. There was a lot to learn. My first lesson was discovering there are states that are considered "surrogacy friendly" or "not surrogacy friendly." New York was in the "not friendly." Surrogacy is not legal in New York unless you're related to the person. I love my cousins, but they're either too old or a hot mess.

My fertility doctor sent me to an agency that he's worked with in Pennsylvania. Okay, whatever you say, Doc. I know there are some crazy Eagles fans out there, but I'm desperate and I had to trust him. When I was trying to get pregnant, I felt like I was in control of my narrative. I took the pill. I did the shot. I went to the doctors. Then when I was pregnant, I was out of my mind but still in control of how I ate and slept. Although it was pretty hard to sleep when I'd only known bad endings. When you hire a surrogate, your anxiety is next level because you are literally not in control. Who is this person? Will she be kind to her body with my baby? Is she a Trump supporter? What will she eat? A real-life surrogate situation isn't like *Baby Mama* with Tina Fey and Amy Poehler where they become fast friends. This ain't that. This is a perfect stranger that lives three hours away in another state but wow, when you've exhausted all your possibilities and there's one more teeny-tiny glimmer of hope, you hold on to that shit like Elián Gonzalez held on to that raft.

I made an appointment. The owner was nice but short and to the point. Her business partner was a five-time surrogate. They were a dynamic duo. These two were boss women in the middle of nowhere facilitating all this, just making dreams come true.

The interview was long. Really long. Like have-to-take-a-break-for-lunch long. They walked us through every possible scenario we could have. There were things they answered that I didn't even think about. Would I want her to hold my baby after it's born? Do I want her to breastfeed? This transaction had to be carefully well thought out, and I don't think that I was in the proper headspace to do that. My husband

and I drove hours to meet these ladies to see if this was something we would want to do with them, but it didn't occur to me that they would be interviewing us as well. That actually made me feel better. They wanted to know if we were worthy candidates. I didn't feel discouraged, but rather hopeful. They kept talking about success stories, but that voice was always in the back of my head, and I kept thinking, *Yeah, right, we'll see, you've tried so hard. Why would it all work out now?*

Well, it turned out they had just interviewed someone who was a worthy candidate that week and she checked all the boxes. She happened to be in the neighborhood, so she stopped by and we met. She was fantastic. Warm and sweet and had a family of her own. She found being pregnant euphoric. Girl, bye, this was everything! It's a rarity to meet someone within the first day, but I thought the universe was on my side smiling down at us and hooking us up on the fast track to having a family because we had waited so long and been through so much. This was my rainbow at the end of the storm. We talked for hours, and before I knew it, it was almost dinnertime! I cut the evening short because Gijs and I had to head back to Brooklyn for a surprise birthday dinner I put together for him. It was his fortieth birthday, and yes, we were going to Holland for his birthday. I tried to set up a little something something for him with his friends in Brooklyn.

When things are rough for me I try to celebrate as much as possible. Obviously you can't forget the hard times you're going through, but it reminds us that there's still stuff to celebrate. We arrived late to the restaurant, but it was perfect because when we rolled up, all our friends were there waiting with balloons. Ten minutes later my friend says, "Oh shit! That guy is dressed like Elvis!" Then it hit me. I forgot I booked an Elvis impersonator for my husband's surprise dinner. I forget a lot of shit all the time. One time I booked us tickets to go see *Misery* on Broadway with Bruce Willis and Aunt Jackie (Laurie Metcalf) and totally forgot about it. I got an email asking how we liked the play. You know you're overwhelmed and exhausted when you're forgetting the fun stuff. By the way, did you know that there's a whole tier of Elvises you can book? There's the cheap one that sort of looks like Elvis and will lip-synch to a song for you. Then there's the dude that will dress up like Elvis, looks like him a bit, but will lip-synch with a dance. But if you wanna treat yourself, there's the dude that will dress up like Elvis and sing to music. Then there's the top-notch dude that is usually in between his Vegas gigs. He walks and talks like Elvis. He'll wear *legit blue suede shoes* and can play a guitar, so you don't need music. That's who I went for. I mean, if you're gonna do Elvis, you might as well not half-ass the king!

We excitedly told our friends about the amazing surro-

You know how sometimes you book an Elvis impersonator for your husband's surprise birthday dinner and then forget you did that? No, just me?

Courtesy of author collection

gate we met. They all raised a glass to extending our family. But the more friends I shared my surrogate news with, the more alone I felt. Why I expected anyone to get what we were doing, I have no idea. None of my crew really knew about IVF. They sort of treated it like Botox. "Oh yeah, I've heard of that expensive procedure; I had an aunt that did it." I told one of my comedian friends about it because she asked how we were doing, and she said, "Wow, aren't you fancy? Spending all that money, that's some rich people shit." As if I'm thinking, *Oh, look at this bish now, I'm the Meghan Markle of* Downton Abbey *with my expensive alternative options for life.* That's not how I felt at all. I felt broken, tired, and defeated. I felt like I was at the end of my rope and wasn't sure that I was ever going to be a mom.

I was floored to be spending every penny me, my husband (and now my parents) have saved. I was thinking, *This baby better be a genius because we can't afford to send them to school.* But you can't go there in conversation. You have to just read the room and decide what is chill or not to share. Even though she made me feel uncomfortable, I decided it was me that had to not embarrass her? So dumb.

I told one friend's husband that we were going with a surrogate and he said, "Oh shit! You cheated!! You can't do that!" I was not amused. I was not cheating. I felt cheated. This was a last-resort effort for us to grow our family, and the fact that I had to apologize for it or explain to anyone why this was important was so ridiculous. Thankfully I had a few supportive friends. One was so sweet and thoughtful. She sent me a handwritten note in the mail. Who does that anymore? She said she didn't know what I was going through but could only imagine how hard it was. She also sent me a clipping of an article that a woman wrote about surrogacy that made me feel less alone. It was about how she couldn't have envisioned this path of uncertainty although isn't that what life is. Would she feel less like a mother because she was not able to carry? That part. I thought about it all the time. I asked my mother if I could see pictures of her pregnant with me. Every child wants to know. What would I show my children? All these concerns seem meaningless when you're talking about a healthy child, but it's so hard to take the emotion out of it because I've learned that being a parent means you run on emotion. Out of all the bullshit my friends said to me over the years of trying, these definitely took the cake:

"Why would you want to bring a child into Trump's America?"

"Well, because I don't live my life based on what old white men do in the world—if I did, I'd never get anything done."

"Why don't you just adopt?"

"We tried to, from multiple places."

"Well, you're going to have a surrogate; will you be breathing like you're giving birth when she's in labor? Like in *Handmaid's Tale?*"

"How about you unfollow our friendship and please get the fuck out of my face with that nonsense."

All I ever needed was "I'm sorry you're going through this. I can't imagine what that's like. If you need a hug let me know." A thoughtful article is the cherry on top.

Two months had passed, and while our surrogate was getting all her tests completed, my family and I were completing the adoption papers for the birth. YOU HEARD ME RIGHT. ADOPTION PAPERS. The wild heat that shot through my body as I signed documents stating I would have to adopt my own flesh and blood and if by one cray chance this woman would decide to keep the baby she could. But our lawyer and surrogacy agent assured us that that never happens. Shit. If there's one thing I know is that I am the person that shit happens to when people are like, "Wow, that never happens."

The day of the transfer finally arrived. The transfer is exactly what it sounds like. The doctor has hopped this woman's body up with hormones to prepare for pregnancy and she'll be implanted with our embryo. I was beyond excited. It was as if I was getting impregnated. Because, technically I was? I got a phone call from the doctor's office. I answered with a huge smile on my face, thinking the nurse would tell me that everything is a go. But that wasn't the case. I could hear it in her voice. She was about to give me some hard news. I knew this tone from previous phone calls. There was a problem with our surrogate; I don't even know what exactly. I stopped listening. I couldn't anymore. How many things could go wrong? How much money were we going to spend? How long could we keep putting ourselves through this shit? Was this ever going to happen? Or would I just have to face the fact that this might never happen?

The ladies at the agency were also disappointed for us. They were very understanding and were all glass half-full about it. They said it was better to find out there was an issue before she was implanted then after and we would've had an even bigger devastating loss. They were absolutely right.

My husband could make sense of it and see the logic. I wasn't there yet. The agency said they had someone else available, but she hadn't completed her testing. I was still so sad I just said yes to everything, signed all the checks, dotted all the i's, crossed all the t's, and just kept it moving, thinking that this wouldn't work out either. They told us about her at the end of November and she wasn't fully approved till March/April to start the process. It felt incredibly long. Our agents wanted to know if we wanted to meet her, but I just couldn't do that to myself again. I had to keep it moving to protect myself. I had given so much to everyone all the time, I felt like there wasn't a piece of me to recover. I threw myself into work.

Even though I wasn't on hormone injections anymore, they were still swimming in my system and I was a hot, steaming emotional mess. And that's when I started booking shit. I really had zero fucks to give. I was waiting in limbo for what the next chapter of my life would look like and it was so painful that I had zero filter when it came to a meeting or audition. There weren't any nerves because it wasn't precious. My nerves were shot for another tier in the department of life. There was work that had to be done: memorize lines for the audition, get dressed and show up to meetings, travel, and do stand-up. It was all a beautiful distraction, but boy, oh boy were there times when I wanted to just curl up on my couch and watch TV/cry/eat/rinse/repeat.

Waiting on a surrogate to come through and not having to deal with a traveling case of needles made me feel like a warrior. I had been through some shit. I was still going through shit. Don't fuck with me and get the fuck out of my way.

I booked a small role in a movie called *Someone Great* on Netflix. I auditioned for a bigger part but didn't get it. I was offered this small "Lady on Subway" role and thought, *Fuck it, it's one day of work in NYC, just go.* The director, Jennifer Robinson, let me improv the fuck out of that scene, which ended up going viral. In one part of the scene I'm crying real tears because Gina Rodriguez's boyfriend broke up with her. That was most of my auditions and acting scenes: I would be crying by the end. I'd cry at least once a day, but I'd do it while I had to say something funny or ridiculous. I never knew when the tears would come. To yell at strangers

"I can't believe you've gotta find new dick!" in public and then cry while doing it, is insanity. I know the winner will always be *Moonlight*, but that's some Oscar-nominated-worthy shit right there.

I ended up booking the *Always Be My Maybe* movie with my friends Ali Wong and Randall Park, which was scheduled to film in Vancouver for a couple of months. I was going to miss my husband but needed to work and have a distraction. I was so happy for it, just beyond ecstatic. I'd always loved Ali, since back when I met her in San Francisco in 2006 (I think . . . I can't really remember space or time when it comes to the formative years of comedy. It's just one big-ass open mic and a pint of seltzer). Of course, around the time that I had to leave for Canada to shoot the movie is when things started to get more serious with the surrogate. She had passed all the tests with flying colors and was going to start hormone treatments to prepare for the transfer. I was so excited but it was time to focus on my job.

I didn't entirely read the description of my character in the email for the *Always Be My Maybe* audition. I skimmed it. Like I said, at that time I was just saying yes to all the dresses. If I would have read it more carefully I would've noticed that I would be playing Ali's best friend, who happens to be very pregnant. What. The. Fuck. I didn't even realize until the stylist on set showed me a rack of maternity clothes. Welp. Okay, universe. I'm fucking here and fucking hear you loud and fucking clear. You wanna go? Let's go.

My wardrobe fitting was surreal. I had to put on a pregnant belly and then try clothes. So many feelings rushed through my body. I was secretly excited to see myself so pregnant. Wow. This is what I would've looked like. I can't see my feet, but I never could anyway, my tits are so big. "Oh, yeah, I'll change the shirt. Sure, yes, yeah, it's not real. This isn't real. This will never be real; it'll never happen. What would it be like if it were real? Would I be here doing this? How big would the baby be?" It was bittersweet.

I took off the belly, and I was sad. I was able to talk myself through it since everything was going so well with the surrogate so far. Back to happy again. I went to work the following day excited to go in my trailer 'cause shit! I was gonna be in a movie that's funny as fuq with these two heroes! I opened my trailer and saw the pregnant belly on a hanger next to my wardrobe. Shit. I've gotta do this a lot. Oh, right, till the end of the movie. I put the belly on, got dressed, and waddled down to hair and makeup. It looked so real that transportation guys were opening doors for me and letting me through. I was already treated so differently. Every day someone would say:

"Wow, you look so good pregnant, do you want to have *your own* babies?"

"Yes."

"When?"

"When you pay for them."

I can't. I've had a ton of realizations going through this

painful process privately as a public person. I'm not going to assume that everyone wants the same things I do. I'm not going to assume that they're doing the things that I'm doing. I'm also not going to cheapen beautiful tragic life moments to elevator talk.

While I was living my best life in Vancouver I was also pretty lonely. Husband and I would talk all day because, well, we're married and also we still had tons of paperwork to do for the surrogacy process. I had to take a look at my life and be like, what the fuck? You're in Vancouver shooting a movie and you've got an escrow account for your surrogate. Who do you think you are? If y'all knew what kind of hot mess I really am you would also be hella surprised that this is happening. I am such a mess. Like walking-into-walls, ripping-my-shirt-on-the-air, I'll-have-the-one-string-that-gets-caught-on-a-Christmas-tree-and-take-it-down-like-a-Griswold-holiday-movie steaming mess. I'm surprised I was able to keep it together on set. I couldn't help but touch this huge pregnant belly all the time. I'd think about the surrogate and then make myself think about something else. And then I think about what I'd name a baby. It was a vicious cycle.

The week we shot my character giving birth was ironically the week that my surrogate was going in for the transfer. It was pretty unbelievable. It was like I got a new phone plan and the universe wants to be on it. I hear you, universe!!! I had some communication with the surrogate as we reached each phase confidently and safely. Shooting that scene in a hospital gown with my wife beside me holding a newborn baby was surreal as fuck. Could the cast and crew see on my face how much I really wanted this?

Two weeks later we found out we were pregnant. I was beside myself. Up until now I was just talking to the agent. She was guiding me through all of it. I finally had to muster up the courage to call this wonderful woman and say thank you. So I did. And she sounded sweet and honest, and I was so happy about that. Thank God she didn't sound mean, impatient, or like she was a former smoker. She seemed genuinely excited, and I didn't know how to thank her enough; I just couldn't stop saying "thank you" over and over again like an emotional, tired broken record of gratitude. How do you start this journey together when you've never been in this seat before? You don't want to overstep boundaries, but you also want to be emotionally and physically available. She said she felt pregnant and also prayed for it. That calmed me down. She also said that she doesn't like spaghetti but was craving pasta. Oh man. I knew this was my child. I love pasta so much I can make it for breakfast, lunch, and dinner. Are you serious? Kraft mac and cheese was the first thing I learned how to cook. Pasta in the morning with sautéed spinach, cut-up turkey bacon, and a fried egg on top? Please. Back. The. Fuck. Up. For the first time in a long time, I felt secure. Could this actually happen?

The stress and anxiety that comes with trying to get pregnant with alternative methods is unreal. It's like you're treating your body like an algebra problem. Then your surrogate finally gets knocked up and wow—there's a whole other set of stress-inducing issues. Is she okay? Is the baby okay? Does she live somewhere with steps? Is she eating enough greens? Is she drinking enough water? Are you sure the babies were craving McDonald's? How do you check in with someone doing something so magical and intimate for you? The things that would race through my mind. Every time I got a text from her my heart would sink, and then when she said everyone's okay my heart would jump. It was an emotional roller coaster at Six Flags.

We finally met at an appointment when she was about four months pregnant. It's strange, I know. And hard to determine what protocol is right or wrong. The surrogacy agent sort of guides you through the dos and don'ts. It was like an out-of-body experience really. She told me I was very hands-on and emotional, which is so funny to hear because I was thinking I hadn't done enough. I wasn't there for every needle she had to endure. Every appointment where she had to put her feet in those dreaded stirrups. Every time she got a cold, or had a pain, or a cramp, I couldn't be there. It was just physically impossible. I had to remind myself constantly to take care of myself and still maintain a relationship with my husband. Hustle in my work life.

At this point in the year I booked *First Wives Club* with Ryan Michelle Bathe and Jill Scott. Another wonderful distraction that couldn't have come at a better time. The catch-22 of the whole situation was that I was unable to attend doctor appointments because I was filming. The doctor appointments I did make it to were pretty much cut-and-dried. I don't know what I expected, but I did feel like an outsider most of the time. My job was pretty much done. The doctor wasn't going to ask questions about me anymore. It's her body, her temple, her life, and I'm just on the sidelines supporting it was an adjustment at first.

Gijs was so supportive; we were totally out of our comfort zone and yet he was so patient. He didn't even come into the room to see a sonogram till she was six months. There's no rhyme or reason why we waited that long. It just felt kinda awkward to have her be half-naked and him in the room. Maybe I made it awkward, but I was just trying to make everyone feel comfortable. Well, her—I wanted her to feel comfortable. Husband and I would try to make sense of it. He expressed that he felt he was missing out and that it would be great if he could at least go in the room to the appointment. I get it. I totally understood. Who knew that this would be us being finally pregnant? Quietly knocking on the door asking if it's okay to come in?

I could not be more grateful for Ryan and Jill while we were filming. They are really my true sister wives; I'm not just saying that. There were times where I had to film with kids. I had kids in the show. Two kids. And my surrogate was pregnant with our *two kids*. Yes. Twins. Our two kids. Our two babies. Our two beating hearts. I didn't know if this was going to work out and if this was all going to happen. I'd break down and cry a lot and Jill and Ryan wiped my tears, held my hands, and prayed over me. When I tell you I didn't know I needed that love and strength, I'm strong enough for everyone, but I did. It was necessary. They fed my soul. They are strong Black women who are boss bitches and mothers. It was the education I didn't know I needed. These women would expect exceptional standards from everyone including themselves but also display this quiet strength that I'm still trying to achieve. I'm so grateful for everyone on *First Wives Club* and then some.

At the wrap party for the show, my friend Mark Tallman, who plays Ryan's character's husband, was there with his wife, who has also been supportive since day one. She asked me how it was all going, and I told her that I was trying to buy breast milk online but the catch is that I had to provide a birth certificate first. That made no sense, and I was pretty upset about it. She'd just had a baby a few months before and said, "Please, I would love to give you my milk." And I cried. I just cried. I still cry about it. When people talk about a village, they're not talking about an assistant or a cousin. They're talking about these people. The doctors, nurses, the surrogate team, the friends and coworkers and people you run into who just do the perfect thing that you didn't know you needed. And now this. Wow. I'm still beside myself when I think about. She gave us milk for almost six months. I couldn't be more grateful.

When twins are born they're considered full term around thirty-two weeks. We were inducing labor at thirty-six weeks. My mother flew into Pennsylvania for the birth, and Husband and I boarded up our home because we didn't know if the babies had to be in the NICU or not. *Nervous* isn't the word. My body felt numb, my jaw would often lock, my right eye had a heartbeat, I had no appetite (THE APPE-TITE THING IS A BIG DEAL), and I could cry at the drop of a hat.

On the big day, it was my surrogate, the agent, my sur-rogate's husband, my mother, and my husband. While she was feeling contractions, there was a moment where we still felt like we couldn't hug and tell her "It'll be okay!" We were still on the sidelines a bit even though we, at this point, had talked a lot, went to a lot of doctor appointments, and had gotten to know each other as well as we could under the cir-cumstances. While she was waiting for the contractions to get bigger, Mom, Husband, and I went next door to have dinner, and we had some wine. I thought, *How did I end up here?* In Pennsylvania, eating dinner at a Holiday Inn, having a glass of merlot while this amazing woman is in labor? Life is so wild. Your journey is never the way you plan, that's for fuck-ing sure, but as long as you're on the journey to getting what you want, who you want, where you want to be, whatever that is, that's all that matters. Whatever you want in your life, I want that for you.

We headed back over to the hospital, and I was numb. Her contractions grew stronger. Because this was a twin birth, it's considered high-risk, so she had to give birth in the OR. Since the OR is small, she was only allowed to have one person with her. We thought she'd choose her husband, but they explained to me that as a mother, you have to be there for the birth of your child. I still feel gobsmacked awful that Gijs couldn't be in the room, but he's so great at keeping his eye on the prize. A lifetime of happiness with these bundles of joy would be enough for him.

I witnessed the most beautiful thing ever.

There were three nurses per baby. Amazing. The doctor was on her twenty-third hour of her twenty-five-hour shift. We were all set up, and we were asking her to push. I didn't feel comfortable yelling, "Push! Push!" like everyone else. Baby girl came right out at 2:46 a.m. She was perfect and beautiful and had curly black hair, and I couldn't believe she was here. She was crying and loud and present. They put her on my surrogate's stomach as they wiped her and asked me to cut the cord. I did. We cried, and I kissed my surrogate on the cheek and said, "Thank you so much." They wheeled little girl away. My heart and mind were all over the place. Is little girl okay? Is little boy okay? What happens next? The doctor immediately said, "Don't push!" Then the nurses started chanting, "Don't push! Don't push!!" And she squealed, "I wanna push!!!!" They yelled back, "DO NOT PUSH!!!!!!!!" I didn't feel comfortable yelling, "Don't push" at her. I kept saying, "Thank you, thank you, you're doing so good, thank you so much." I wish I would've jumped in there, but that didn't feel like it was my place.

The doctor closed her eyes and put both her hands into the surrogate. After what seemed like FOREVER, without even saying anything or opening her eyes, she just nodded her head. And just like that the nurses took her cue and screamed, "Push!!!! Push!!!!!!" I held on to the surrogate's hand. Wondering how baby girl was doing and hoping baby boy would come out alive. And so he did. At 3:00 a.m. on the dot my baby boy came out, and he looked exactly like his sister. Curly black hair, screaming at the top of his lungs, so much personality. The nurses wheeled him off after I cut his cord as well. Baby boy was breeched, but the doctor said nothing and just turned him around. And just like that: my life was changed forever. I saw this woman, no longer a stranger but a member of our village, out of the kindness and goodness of her heart and soul give birth naturally to our twins, Hazel and Otis. I cry every time I think about it. I think about it every day.

To say it's been a struggle is not enough. It's been a ride. A war. A mountain. And I am so glad that I'm on the other side of it. What I can only describe as a black fog of sadness and uncertainty for so very long. To want something so bad in life and be so out of control. To be so sad and then so fulfilled is beautiful mind-fuckery. There's a quote I saw that I love:

"The things you need to survive are not the tools you'll need to survive."

I am forever changed. Reality has finally sunk in. They're here. I'm finally a mother.

I can never die.

MOTHERHOOD

Every time I see a commercial and they say the word *motherhood*, it's spoken in a whisper. It's a romantic, beautiful, lifelong sweet story summed up in just three syllables. Considering I've spent more time trying to be a mother than actually being a mother, I'm not sure I'm qualified to speak on this subject. See, I had my kids "later in life" and having lived in New York City most of my adult life, I understand women who don't really feel the desire to have kids. I don't judge. Just because you don't have a kid doesn't mean that you're not mothering someone. I've mothered friends, family, coworkers, and even my parents from time to time. I'm so tired of the fucking shame people, particularly women, get for not wanting kids. IT IS HER BODY, AND THEREFORE IT IS HER CHOICE. When I'd go out with my husband people would never ask him when he wanted to have kids. But they'd sure as hell ask me. After a while of being asked the same dumb questions about my body, I finally shut them up by offering to send the results of my latest pap smear.

This is the definition of a mother on Wikipedia: "A mother is a female parent which gives birth to the baby after bearing and nurturing the baby in her womb for a period of nine months." Cool. So I guess because I had a surrogate, I'll tell my kids to start calling me "Miss Michelle"? Wikipedia and the general public—we need to update our definition of what motherhood is.

Taking care of newborn twins feels like I'm one of the birds in Sully's jet engine. I'm just going along my merry way enjoying the cool breeze from the Hudson River and then all of a sudden BAM! I'm totally sucked into this metal wheel and just trying to survive. I'm like a shoe in a dryer on a hard tumble dry, stumbling through life. *Ba-boom. Ba-boom. Ba-boom.* That's me trying to wipe my ass, wash my hands, make bottles, and change diapers before a rash occurs on both of their bottoms. It feels like I'm a coach everyone hates, but my team is winning. Or perhaps that I'm a coach everyone loves, but our team is losing. The point is, it's never perfect.

Motherhood adds to my life. It makes me feel important in a way that I've never felt before. People have depended on me, but not in this way. To stay alive, to provide shelter. For guidance on, well, everything. Being a parent is one of the most important jobs ever. Why don't we treat it like that? Whether you've had a planned pregnancy or not, why don't we treat childcare as one of the most important things ever? Parenthood should be offered as a major in college, vocational schools, damn near every school everywhere. Who cares about accounting and social studies? We're just gonna google history or go to an accountant anyway.

For some reason, I thought when I finally got to bring babies home, that's when I'd be able to relax. Oh, bitch, please. There is a whole new wave of momma bear/porky pig (yes you're so tired you can't find pants) anxiety that comes with bringing home teeny, tiny, helpless, gorgeous, please-don't-drop-the-baby, bundles of joy.

The first time I met them was wild. I had an idea in my head how they might look and sound, then I saw them and it's nothing like I thought. It's strange. They're like little aliens that look a bit like you. There was a moment when I really saw them up close and thought, "Shit, I hope you like me. I hope I like you. Let's try to get through this thing called life," and then I started singing "Let's Go Crazy" by Prince in a baby voice.

With one baby, you have to think fast all day long. With twins, you're just running on instinct and emotion. You're an octopus, you're Daniel Day-Lewis in *My Left Foot*. You're the chef at the end of an episode of *Chopped* throwing flatware and garnishes every which way to get your stuff on a plate. These babies are making noises you've never heard before and can't recognize. *Does this sound mean that they're choking? I don't remember the baby CPR video. I should look it up on YouTube. Wait, does that sound mean they're hungry? Okay, I fed them on a hundred-dollar pillow made for specifically feeding twins at the same time, but they're still crying. I think that's a cry. Are they crying because they haven't burped? Oh no, they haven't taken a shit today, or yesterday. How do I burp two little babies at the same time who can't hold their necks up? And if I leave one alone to take care of the other one, will that one have to go to therapy for abandonment issues? This ain't a game! It's a panic room, and where's the next clue? Are they overheated? Warm enough? Oh wow, her neck is hot, and it looks like she's sweating; is she sweating or is this a fever? Oh, right, that baby is sleeping and the other one is about to sleep. Oh shit! Both babies are sleeping. This is a good time for me to sleep. FUCK, why can't I sleep? Why am I just staring at the wall? What did I just do? I can't remember what I just did. Oh, whoops, I just made coffee. That's probably why I can't sleep.*

That was my first day home.

It was really hard for me to sleep when the babies were home with us. I was also going through the whirlwind of being a new mom to premature babies in the dead of winter. But I also feared that if I went to sleep, I wouldn't wake up. Who would take care of them?

I remember Gijs and I just rocking babies back and forth on the couch, staring at each other. We sounded like a scene from *The Hateful Eight*. I asked him one night, "Who's gonna go out for provisions?" There's an incredible pull toward future-thinking I just never experienced before.

I legit couldn't sleep one night because when they were

three days old, I was worried about their first day of school. I want to know what they're gonna look like when they're older. I want them to come to me with their problems and hopefully they'll like me enough so we can figure it out together. I imagined them screaming "I hate you!" as teenagers and slamming the door. Or maybe they are more calm and we can have some *Gilmore Girls* moment where we just talk and talk and talk about their woes till we're blue in the face, and that'll be just enough.

I want them to save me in their phones as "Mommy" even when they're way too old to do that. Like waaaay too old. When they're adults I want their faces to light up at a dinner party when they talk about me and share a story that we had from their childhood where I did something very crazy and it taught them a valuable lesson. PSYCHO, YES? 100 PERCENT PURE LOVE? YES. 1,000 PERCENT.

And, of course, like anything in life, you can prepare yourself to be the best, be on point, read all the books, hear all the stories, but until you've spent a day in those parenting shoes, how the fuck are you going to know what you're doing? Ya just don't, generation to generation. Being a parent, you can't help to think of the relationships you have with your own.

My mother is a good mother. She is always running around doing the most for everyone else, which is so generous, but she's also generous to a fault. She is always so busy bending over backward and forward for everyone else. My mother worked a lot when I was growing up. She was a customs broker. She worked really hard to make partner, but it never happened. Her voice is high-pitched and delicate, and lots of people don't take her seriously, but she relays facts that no one else can fuck with. Therefore she is always hired to make some basic dude look good. She reminds me of Tess (Melanie Griffith's character) in *Working Girl*. She's got the chops, but in a time when you had to be single and childless for people to take you seriously. I'm really proud of my mother and the way her mind works. I don't resent her for not being home. She made sure I was always okay.

I always loved hanging out with my friends' African American moms, because they were like TV-sitcom moms. No-nonsense, tell-it-like-it-is, hey-girl-hey, don't-do-that-girl, advice-show moms. My friends' white moms were cool-ass soccer moms who'd have all the good snacks and had just let themselves go a bit. They all looked like Kathy Bates in *Fried Green Tomatoes* and were usually named Nancy, Ann Marie, or Kimberly. Anything ending in an "ee." I was so here for it.

My mom had style. She looked like she could've been a neighbor of Diana Ross, but she'd be the one neighbor that didn't realize how smart and beautiful she was herself. My mother is very humble, silent, strong. Most people take her kindness for weakness, which makes me yell at them on her behalf. I think she's proud of me even though we're so opposite. I think about Lisa Bonet and Zoë Kravitz's relationship all the time. They just look so chill, like they're always on the same page. How? How is that even possible? I've always been curious about what that's like, to be raised by someone who doesn't worry about what people think.

My mother was raised by her grandmother, Hazel, and *she* was a bad-ass bitch. She was a tiny Indian woman in Jamaica who learned how to hide her burning cigarette in her mouth because smoking was frowned upon. She was a spitfire: honest, direct, and everyone loved her. She lived to be 103.

My mother's mom was named Mavis Louise. She was a big, beautiful Black woman with an Afro and a sturdy gait. Everyone called her Mrs. D. She could light up a room with her laughter and positivity. Her food was so damn good people still talk about it. In fact, that's how she met my white French grandfather. He was in Jamaica and bought food from her, and I guess he decided that he wanted to keep eating from her pot. She had five kids from her husband and would take in kids and young adults from the street and take care of them. That's the Jamaican way. Take care of your own.

Being an only child and raising twins? I can't even pretend to understand what it's like to have two beaming different personalities that will need different love and care and attention. Baby boy Otis is walking sunshine and loves to make eye contact with people so he can share a smile with them. He's got a light in his eyes that's so pure. My little Hazelnut, named after her great-great-grandmother, is similar to who I remember her namesake to be. Smart, thoughtful, doesn't suffer fools, doesn't need to smile at anyone, has her people call your people. I want them to question authority—even mine. I want them to be able to make decisions for themselves and to trust their instincts. Every child should know that their voice is valid.

MOTHERING TO SMOTHERING

For a hot minute I wouldn't take the twins anywhere. I'm not talking about one baby, I'm talking 'bout two. Come on, are you serious? I don't have enough hands to get all that done, and how would I? For the first few months, I felt like I was living two lives. I'd go out and do what I had to do workwise: run errands, regular run-of-the-mill shit. Then I would come home and be a mom. I didn't know how to go out in public and do both.

Then the dreaded day came when I had to travel in an airport with these cutie-pie nuggets. My father wasn't doing so well, and my mother begged us to bring the babies down to Florida. It's really a short flight, so Husband and I did all the research when it came to flying with twins, and we made that shit happen. I'mma let you know now! Nothing makes you feel like you've earned your stripes in parenthood more than traveling with babies, children, or your pet. It's pretty polarizing. People make no bones about what category they fall into. You're either pro-life or pro-quiet. People who are baby-friendly on flights could be a male or female, but either way, without a doubt, they have a kid or are trying to. Then there are the other motherfuckers who are selfish cunts, and they can't believe that you've decided to leave your place and put your babies in their lives. On a flight to Florida to see my parents, Husband and I each had a baby. This guy next to us decides to make a video and say, "Jesus Christ, look at all these fucking babies on my flight." As he panned to us, Husband and I both held up our middle finger in his video, and that's romance, y'all. Please get over yourselves and realize that life happens with or without you. I've worked and prayed very hard to complain about this, I'm so happy that I can!

EVERY PARENT'S WISHLIST

When you see that mom struggling to fold her gahtdamn stroller while her baby is screaming, and she's trying not to drop the bag of groceries in her other hand, with stains all over her clothes, hair tangled, breath stank—that's not who she wants to be in that moment. And that's okay. We all have shit days; let's own it. Every parent has their wish list. I wanna be that mom that brings her kids onstage or on set but then also shows up to all the PTA meetings with a Pinterested peanut-free, dairy-free snack that everyone can get behind. I wanna wake up an hour before everyone else does in the house so I can have me time and work out and be the healthiest version for my kids. I wanna be on some Cicely Tyson shit, where my kids will be like "Can you believe that she looks that good at eighty-five?" I want to be doing the electric slide at my ninetieth birthday with my kids on either side of me just like, "Wow! My mom is so inspired!" I want when I'm long gone that my kids still have a tear in their eye because they're proud when they speak of me. I'd love my children to look back at my career and think, *Damn, my mom was a bad-ass bitch who lived a full life and worked hard to have us here by any means necessary. My mother not only made crazy, bold choices in life, she also taught us so many valuable lessons.* Maybe this is just a little too hopeful. But sometimes the only thing we have is our imaginations, and if we don't hope for anything, then how can we expect anything good to happen?

Cue RuPaul: "If you can't love yourself, how the hell you gonna love someone else? Now don't fuck it up."

TAKE ME TO CHURCH

I grew up Catholic. I mean really, really Catholic. In fact, to say I just "grew up Catholic" is an understatement. Catholic is my nationality. The way some people are "culturally" Jewish, that for me is Catholicism. Because my family is Caribbean, I've learned that the poorer the country, the more religious the people. If you're still thinking, "Michelle, I've seen your act. How Catholic can you really be?" Well, let me tell you how Catholic. Seriously, all dick jokes aside—I'm talking like archbishop-in-the-family Catholic. I mean twelve-years-of-Catholic-school Catholic. Sure, there are lots of folks who are Irish, Italian, Hispanic, et cetera, with a priest or two in the family. If you have a family member who is (or was) a cop or a firefighter, then you probably have an uncle who is a priest. I get it. I understand Martin Scorsese films. But, I see your priest and I raise you an archbishop. Name someone else who has a Jamaican archbishop for their uncle. You can't. Jamaican Rasta, sure. But Jamaican, Roman Catholic archbishop?

I win, hands down. We'll get back to the archbishop in a minute.

My mom and my dad also grew up pretty Catholic. My mom wanted to be a nun, and my Haitian dad was an altar boy. We were always at church. We were either at a Jersey mass or, when we went back to my mom's people in Jamaica, we were hitting up the Jamaican church services. My Jamaica trips were never what people imagined. Friends automatically assumed that I was gonna be on a beach getting my hair braided and sipping coconut drinks. Yeah, it wasn't that. Usually my mother and I would stay in a convent so we could go to mass at 6:00 a.m. Jamaican churches are so different. Everyone is happy even though they don't have much. Everybody knows one another. They'd congregate after mass for tea and cake. The church had the bare minimum decor. These Jamaican churchgoers were so happy for even just a fan to blow on them, an open window, and a tambourine to play God's music. It's a different life.

Jersey church, on the other hand, is just what you'd think it would be. Picture a mix of very tired moms with Kate Gosselin haircuts (season one, the aggressive years) next to a bunch of dull dads in wrinkled khakis. The truth is, I always wished for an upbringing in a Black church. Something real Baptist and Madea-like. I often walk by Black churches in Brooklyn and it looks like a party. Everyone's got their hands in the air, clapping, testifying, shaking, jumping, and wearing their best outfits. The choir alone is reason enough to join a

Baptist church. You mean everyone in the choir is just sounding like Jennifer Hudson naturally? I'd turn my chair around for that. All that Black church swag versus a Roman Catholic service, which is like a Costco demo pitch if I'm being honest, and there's just no contest. The Black church is the God sorority I'd pledge first. The Roman Catholic congregation is just a lot of very tired people selling a product you're not really sure they believe in. It's just habits from way back, so they keep doing it like that "TV dinners at five o'clock" routine that happens right before you go to forever sleep in that La-Z-Boy recliner.

I'm not saying you shouldn't do you. I'm not saying there aren't good Catholics. Heck (see how I did that), there's my uncle: he's a good Catholic. This man knew he was called to the Church from a very young age. As my mother tells it, "He knew he wanted to be a priest from the time he was a little boy. At fifteen, he tried to enter the seminary, but they thought he was too young and they didn't accept him. His love of God, spreading the word of God, and helping the poor and marginalized are his greatest passions." Well, that's a "calling" in every sense of the word. He also loves history, writing, preaching, and traveling. It's not the first place guidance counselors recommend, but you do get all that as an archbishop. So, for my uncle, it's everything. That kind of commitment and passion, I respect it. Plus, there's a beauty to ritual. That ritual, conditioning, and a need to search for something higher than myself are all reasons that I've continued going to church, even solo, as an adult. Yet even with the best of intentions and a desire to live true to my roots, things don't always work out.

What do I mean? Well, for example, one time I went to Saint Paul's in New York City and I sat behind this homeless dude with a shitty butt. I know it was a shitty butt because it kept playing peekaboo during the service like Hershey's highway to hell. It was so hard not to focus on this poor man and his super-dirty butt during the service. Homeboy also knew more words to the hymns than I did. Damn, just as I'm thinking all that, he starts digging back into his butt like the Hershey Highway is on fire and he has got to smother it with his dirty, dirty digits. Then, of course, we reached that point in the service where you say "Peace be with you" and you're supposed to shake your neighbor's hand. God help me. Is shaking his hand the Christian thing to do, even if I might get a parasite and don't have health insurance? I know Jesus spent a lot of time with the lepers, but I'm guessing he probably bathed them off first, and I don't even have a Handi Wipe or Purell. This is a test. It's a test by the Almighty and I am failing, big-time. Homeless dude reaches out his hand. I fake a wave. Shit, did Jesus see that? Well, Jesus, help a girl out! Have her remember the Handi Wipes or send a Jesuit down to bathe this poor man before "peace be with you." Why it gotta be all on me? But, when you're a Catholic, it is totally. All. On. You.

Take the "Catholic camp" I had to go to with my husband before we got married. Or the shoulder caps I had to add to my sleeveless wedding dress, because some dude might get a boner looking at my shoulders, and therefore MY FAULT. It's the lady's fault, always. I think that's written in the Bible: "When in doubt, blame a lady!" Peter: 16:19. Okay, that ain't real. But, truly, isn't it God's fault even once though? He gave me fine shoulders after all, so why do I got to cover 'em up? I'm just calling it like I see it. Okay, back to "Catholic camp," bye.

When you get married in the Catholic Church, you have to go to Christian marriage boot camp. It's a weekend where you hang out with other couples who are about to get married in the Church. Now, my husband is an atheist. I don't think he realized what he was getting into by marrying me and my religiously and culturally Catholic family. We wanted to get married on a beach. We love the beach, but the archbishop had to marry us, and a beach isn't a house of God, so we had to find a church. So, here my hubby-to-be found himself at a Catholic marriage boot camp with me. I could tell from his face that he didn't understand why we had to complete Catholic sleep-away camp to get married in a church. I had no answer for him, and to add insult to injury, the men and women had to sleep in different buildings. WHAT. THE. FUCK. YEAR. IS. IT?? We also had to do these different activities and check them off when they were completed. You would think with my uncle being the archbishop we could skip the line at the deli counter, but no. One activity included writing a prayer about our life together. We could barely get through a shopping list at Trader Joe's when that was real life, how in the heck were we gonna do this? Then we had to wait in a long line to tell our newly written prayer to the priest. My man doesn't like to do karaoke even after a few tequila shots! But we got through it and it wasn't all bad. The teachers were couples that were married forty-plus years. I tried to get into it, and so did my man. But ultimately, the prison cots and jailhouse shower shoes got the best of us. We did our time and got the hell out. I still look back at that and can't believe what my atheist man did for me. It was a lot to ask, but he did it anyway.

If we had an NBC show about our wedding, it would be called *This Is NOT Us*. It's on Tuesday nights at 9:00 p.m. . . . and every single night after that: till death do us cancel. But until then, WE GONNA DO US.

CATHOLIC ROYALTY

When I found out that my uncle the priest was going to be ordained as an archbishop in Rome, Husband and I said we're so broke, but we have to go! This is the closest thing to royalty! We were beaming with pride for my uncle and all his hard work. Seeing as we had no money, I booked us on a real cheap flight to Rome. It was a great price, but we did have to make three connecting flights between New York and Rome with only a ten-minute layover between each flight.

By layover number two, as Husband and I ran from terminal to terminal, I realized I should've worn an exercise bra if I was going to be doing CrossFit all day. I also wanted to have my big, churchy fashion moment, so I bought one of those epic church-lady hats. I was looking for something reminiscent of *The Color Purple* or *Steel Magnolias*, big and lacy with Southern charm, yet real churchy feeling. I was sprinting all over each airport with my titties jiggling and my big-assed church hat trailing behind me like I had just snatched Madea's wardrobe and I was trying to outrun the po-po. It was madness, but we finally arrived in Rome only to find out that our luggage said *Fuck this* three flights ago and parked itself in Frankfurt, Germany, for a bratwurst and a pint. Damn. When your luggage gives up, you know you bought a cheap flight.

Worn out and resigned to wearing my panties inside out (don't act like you've never done it) till I could get my bag back, we dragged ourselves to the hostel I booked. Our hostel had me feeling real "hostile" within five minutes. It was so small that Husband and I had to do the electric slide around each other to even get to the bathroom. Not to mention this bathroom was so small that all four sides of my body were touching the walls when I was on the toilet or in the shower. And when I showered, the toilet was in said shower with me like a shitty friend mocking me for my pathetic bank account. But we made do biding our time with touristy stuff and family events until the big day.

Every member of my family came to Rome for the ordination. My mom, dad, her brothers, half brothers, cousins, peripheral family, people we just met on 23andMe who said they were cousins, coworkers, and friends. From my family, there were eighty people alone. Plus we brought my comedian friend Eric Andre. He's part Haitian and part Jewish. We used to get booked to do the road together a lot, because people thought we were related. So real quick he became the brother I never wanted but grew to love. Eric was just starting to pop in the business, and his show was taking off when we invited him to Rome and the ordination. He had some college friends in Rome, and they took us around for overpriced artisanal cocktails and showed us the real Rome that only locals know. Every now and again we'd hit up Eric's sweet Airbnb too. It was biiiiig compared to our hostel, and it had real plumbing. It made me understand what making it in the business could really get you. We all had to go shopping, because my luggage hadn't arrived and Eric didn't own a suit. So he bought his first designer suit, which I could tell he loved. It was like he had "I am an international spy" written all over his face. I kept praying our luggage would come because I truly had no money. Every time I called the airlines they kept saying it was "Saint Paul's" holiday or "Saint Joseph's" or "Saint Peter's" and people have the day off, so there's nobody available to look for my damn luggage. I was like, "Jesus Christo, is there a Patron Saint of Clean Panties I can pray to or like a Saint of Lost Lufthansa Luggage?" Yep, it was time to "let go and let

God" as far as my luggage was concerned, so I bought an affordable (cheap) dress at a drugstore. But don't worry about me, honey. I paired that thang with my overpriced church hat and I was Tyler Perry–movie ready.

When Husband and I weren't hanging out with Eric, we were meeting up with our eighty relatives after sightseeing. Now, people assume that religious folks have their shit together. Truth be, they don't! We'd meet up with my aunts and uncles from Staten Island, and I'd ask them how they liked the Colosseum. My aunt would say, "Meh, it's under construction. There's no baked chicken or jousting, and ya uncle with his gout and all them steps? Meh, overrated." So, let me get this straight. This monumental structure, built in 70–80 AD (AD, BITCH!), and you don't like that it's dilapidated and needs maybe a spruce up? Nah, hard pass.

Ordination day arrived and it was hella hot. About fifteen hundred Catholic folks, including eighty of my relatives, my hubby, Eric, and I were crammed into a cheap-seats section of Saint Peter's Basilica. There was no air-conditioning. It's like an act of contrition just attending something at the basilica during the summer. I was feeling really sweaty, and also like Tom Hanks in *Angels & Demons* looking around for the Illuminati or the Holy Grail, when the ceremony started. Forty bishops from all over the world were being ordained, so the ceremony was in multiple languages, a key one being Latin. The whole thing felt like the opening ceremony of the Olympics to me. I couldn't understand a thing, and then suddenly I'd hear, "And now, Guatemala!" Within seconds, dozens of iPads would fly up into the air like a sea of Moses wannabes holding up the tablets of the commandments.

My uncle got ordained. It made him as happy as can be, which is a good thing because he's a good man. I'd even say he's the glue that holds the family together. No matter how immature anyone gets (and that happens with family), my uncle tends to bring them back around. Usually what happens is someone says something off-putting and no one wants to talk to them for a couple of years. But then my uncle will bring everyone back together through different religious events. He'll say something like, "I just opened an orphanage for disabled infants and kids" or "I just started up this AIDS hospice. Come and celebrate the opening with me," and just like that all the family members are talking and celebrating as a family again. We're living in a world where there are definitely bad priests, and the Vatican has not done the best job in dealing with those atrocities or helping a lot of hurt Catholics really recover. But my uncle, he's one of the good ones, and he's trying to do the right thing.

The truth is, I still really struggle with what I believe. But I do believe in kindness and in supporting good people. So while I may never have a "Your Majesty" in the family, I do have a "Your Excellency." Thankfully, I was there to see it all go down. Glory be, bish!

A FABULOUS BLESSING

When I had my twins, the first question my mother asked me was, "Will they be baptized?" Husband and I agreed that we wouldn't do things just for my parents anymore. From the wedding on out, it was him and me doing our thing, for *us*. But I figured if getting baptized helps their little souls and gives a person a spiritual head start in this crazy world, then I wasn't opposed to doing it. Plus, it was an excuse to throw a party for my beautiful twins. I had waited so long for them that I was looking forward to Pinteresting the shit out of a new baby soiree! Now, I was busy as all get-out with a new movie career happening, an hour comedy special to work out, a big move to a new part of the city for me and my family, and this *here* book you're reading, but still . . . if I was gonna do it: I was gonna do it, do it. So I had it catered. I bought a five-hundred-dollar cake with a huge crucifix on it. It was beautiful, that cake. It was très Cathy. And, of course, who was going to perform the baptism? None other than my archbishop uncle.

Husband and I thought long and hard about who we wanted the godparents to be. We wanted them to be our chosen family. Friends who knew my parents, so when they were gone, they could tell our babies stories about who they were. Friends who knew us for a long time and were still hanging strong as part of our community. Now, Husband was never baptized in the Catholic Church, even though his brothers and sisters were. I guess by the time he arrived, my mother-in-law had given up on all that. Gijs never cared that he wasn't baptized, and neither of us believe it makes you less of a good human. However, as a kid, Gijs did want a set of godparents. So much so that he self-appointed his neighbor to be his godfather. I'm not sure the neighbor had a choice in the matter. Gijs just decided that was his godfather. Every time report cards came around, little Gijs would be at the fence going, "*Peetvader* [godfather in Dutch], come and look at my grades, *Peetvader*." It was so damn cute. It also made me realize my kids are probably going to want some god-parents. So we really put some thought into it. I also picked two godmoms who are gay. Knowing the Church, I called my mom and said, "The godmoms are gay. Is that going to be a problem?" She said, "Let me check," which made me feel gross because, you know, the Church doesn't have a stellar record as of late. I'm always walking a tightrope when I think about being part of an organization that protects child mo-lesters. Mom came back and said, "Everything's going to be okay. Just relax. You worry too much. Why bring bad stuff up when there's so much to celebrate?" I believed her.

The week before the baptism was my birthday. I de-cided to rent a place up in Woodstock, New York, for me, Husband, the godmoms, and my twins. My thought was, "Let's bring chosen family together each year so my kids can know them and we can all be together." My godmoms were Terri, my coworker from my late-shift-at-NBC days way back, and Rebecca, one of my longtime stand-up comedian friends. Rebecca brought her wife, Kari, who is a veterinarian. Rebecca kept calling herself "the GM" for "Godmom" and Kari "the GMA" for "Godmom Adjacent." I thought it was hella cute and shit. I was getting two for the price of one in the sister-wives category. Bargain hunter! Husband, gay godmoms/sister wives and I were loving the hell out of Woodstock. There was a pool and we were enjoying swimming with the babies and just hanging out. One time, when I had my babies out there poolside, there was a snake by the pool! A snake! I didn't sign up for no snake shit! Girl, BYEEEE! Kari and Rebecca snake-charmed that shit back into the woods while I ran clutching my two babies right back into the house. Did you hear me? They snake-charmed that shit! I don't know if they used the long arm of the pool skimmer or a Wiccan incantation, but I do know they cleansed the reptiles right outta that pool and made it safe for my babies. Yep, they handled that shit like Sam Jackson and Julianna Margulies in *Snakes on a Plane*!

Birthday weekend came to an end, and we headed back to the city for the baptism ceremony. Kari and Rebecca had rented a couple of Airbnbs in Brooklyn, but one of them had a real late check-in, so Rebecca asked if they could drop their luggage off at my house. I said of course, and as luck (or divine providence) would have it, Rebecca and Kari were going to be dropping off their luggage at the exact same time that the archbishop, my mom, and all my Jamaican relatives would be pulling up. My mom called me from the car and said, "When we get there, is Becky going to be there? Can you not introduce Kari as her wife when we arrive?" I felt my body get hot from head to toe and I said, "Absolutely not." The only thing I'm going to do now *is* introduce her as Becky's wife, because that's exactly who she is!

The family entered like a church bus unloading at a free barbecue, and my lesbian sister wives were already there holding their godchildren and smiling. So you know what happens next—I did what I had resolved to do. I introduced Rebecca's wife as her fuckin' wife! Trust, if I went somewhere in Holland and someone told Gijs *not* to introduce me as his wife, you best believe heads would be rolling. It was a real pregnant moment when I did it, but then it passed. Everyone acted nice, polite, cordial, and excited for the baptism the next day.

Perfect, I thought. Love can win.

About two hours later, as I was getting my hair did, archbishop uncle called me on the phone. "Are you sitting down?" he asked.

"Yes, it's my favorite thing to do," I answered.

Uncle: I have to tell you, the church only recognizes the union between a man and a woman.
Me: Uh-huh? And?
Uncle: It does not recognize two women. So I'm sorry, but I will not be able to perform the christening.

Me: But I have a five-hundred-dollar cake. What am I supposed to do? I don't get it. I have people coming from all over. I told Mom they were gay.

Uncle: I'm sorry, I can't.

Me: Why is it not okay? Oh my God, are you serious? You can't be serious. But it's legal in this country.

Uncle: But it's not legal in the Church.

Me: They were straight when I met them eighteen years ago. Is there a loophole?

Uncle: I'm really so sorry, Michelle, I did not make the rules; perhaps call on someone else that's married?

Me: Or my friend that's known me forever?

I got off the phone and called an emergency family meeting with Mom and Husband. My mom was like, "I told you not to introduce them as a couple! I can stand there for them, and they can just sit and watch and we can just do it."

But I just couldn't.

I was all over the place. Do I try to make my mother happy? My uncle happy? Do I believe my babies are going to hell if I don't do this? Is that what they (the Church) want me to believe?

My husband said, "I don't need to do this." He said he

was just "doing it for me." That's why I love him so much. He's not pressuring me to do something I don't want to do or be something I'm not. My mom and I argued for a while, and she cried. I never want to hurt my mom, but I just couldn't see baptizing my babies without my friends. I just couldn't do it. So instead I started to panic. I called the catering company and explained why we had to move the place, again. They were amazing. They comped my delivery fee. I called around throwing a literal "Hail Mary" pass at some other churches to see if they would do the service, which was supposed to be tomorrow. Doing it at my house would be challenging, because there was a Brooklyn block party on my street the next day, and where would everyone park? In my frantic state, I talked to my calm friend Jessica and explained what had happened. She said, "Well, what if we do a blessing? My husband is an officiant with the State of New York, and we could throw a program together if that's okay?"

If that's okay? OMG, all I was thinking is, *I am so lucky for these friendships, and how do I honestly thank these people?* It's true, you realize who your real people are when you really need them. Those are your people. Hold 'em close! I spent the night texting and emailing everyone our Brooklyn address.

The next morning, I got up and I had no idea how I was going to fix our house for a huge soiree. It just wasn't ready. But my friends Bethany and Josh came over and arranged the place like it was the day after a house party in every eighties movie and my parents were about to come home! Bethany did my living room like a *People* magazine wedding with white candles and mason jars everywhere, and Josh just happened to have an entire PA system in his car for the ceremony. (Comedians, you gotta love 'em. They travel with mics and speakers.) It was quickly going from canceled-baptism-from-hell to BLESSING FROM HEAVEN.

Everyone arrived pretty much knowing the story. So there was a sense of kumbaya and "We will bless these babies!" It was like we were at a Bernie rally and he just mentioned college was gonna be free for everybody! The blessing was beautiful—dare I say, it was fabulous. There wasn't a dry eye in the house. The guests said to me again and again, if God was anywhere today, He was here. I felt so happy for my two perfect souls that I was so fortunate enough to have blessed by a really incredible group of family and friends. The only person who cried out of sadness was my mom in the corner. She was looking like Trump won the election all over again, so I asked her if she was okay.

She said, "No, how could you choose your friends over your family?"

I said, "I didn't. I chose right over wrong."

Becoming a parent, I've realized that you have to parent yourself first. (My friend Jordan told me that.) There's no way I'd be able to look at my children years from now and tell them, "Well, I went along to go along." I can't take the easy way out, because I don't want them to do that. I want them to question the status quo. I want them to decide for themselves. I don't want them to judge someone for their sexual orientation, but instead "by the content of their character." That's the creed we should live by. That's what makes us beautiful. And if I'm lucky enough to have a gay child? Then I'm blessed, just like I'm blessed right now: fabulously blessed.

The family and chosen family I am fabulously blessed to have.

Photo by Mindy Tucker

A LIGHT LOAD

As a light-skinned Black woman I don't wake up every day hoping someone will tell me how Black I am. But there are lots of people out there who are up for the challenge. They look at me, often lowballing my blackness percentage and then talk shit about Black people to me because they've decided, "Well, she's really not that Black." I may have put on a couple of pounds this year but, boo, your ignorance is weighing me down. Being Black is so much more than having dark skin. It is a feeling. It is pride. It is your soul. It is food. It is music. It is culture. I AM A PROUD BLACK WOMAN, AND YOU ARE TALKING SHIT ABOUT MY PEOPLE. LEAVE ME BE.

Sometimes I truly have more respect for flat-out racist motherfuckers than the subtle census taker. One time I was out with my dad in South Florida, trying to pick up some rotisserie chicken for dinner. (And the sides. Dear LAWD the sides!) We were in a pretty busy parking lot, and I was trying to make my parents' Mazda minivan work in this small-ass parking space, so I was taking my sweet old time. This white dude in a big-ass pickup truck—who was probably a real-life juror in *A Time to Kill*—yelled out his window, "Learn how to park you fat nigger!!!" I was pretty taken aback. I asked my dad, "Now why did he have to call me fat?" My dad said, "Well, at least he knows you're Black."

Growing up in bumble-fuck Jersey and then South Florida in the nineties, I was pretty used to hearing the N-word. It was like a Spike Lee movie. I was used to my friends saying it to one another. I was used to white and Spanish people getting mad at me and yelling it. This wasn't that long ago, but it was a different culture. This was before #MeToo, before #BlackLivesMatter, before the internet and phones with cameras. Oh man, you couldn't go to Facebook to find the dude that yelled "fat nigger" at you in the parking lot and then find his ass, only to see that he's a choir instructor who's about to be fired. Nope. There was no Shaun King posting, protecting, and defending us. We only had these stories for dinner parties or some sort of social setting, and we had to keep it moving. And before you come for me, yes, this is an essay about being Black, and yes, I started this shit with my buying some chicken. I AM NOT ASHAMED.

One thing most white people don't understand is something called colorism. Colorism is discrimination against individuals with a dark skin tone, typically among people of the same ethnic or racial group. Plain and simple? It's the light versus dark. Having light skin isn't a choice. It's not like

I went to Build-A-Bitch. My mother is half white. Her father was from France. My father is a browned-skinned Haitian who has vitiligo. So yeah, we next-level bright. The assumption is because I'm light I think I'm better than someone with dark skin, and I'd like to leave that old-school bullshit with the trash.

I've had people ask me if I could get along with Black women who have darker skin than mine. This shit makes me so sad. I can't express how sad. I've spent years crying about it. Black folks tend to think that everyone would love to look like Terrence Howard, but that's not the case. Melanin is beyond gorgeous, and you're lucky if you have it. My family is all shades and sizes, and that's what makes us beautiful. I will not let this oppressive bullshit standard set by colonial white men ruin my relationships with my beautiful brothers and sisters. I'm fucking done. Jesus Christ on High, can we take Black the night and celebrate ourselves by any means possible instead of picking us apart? If we fight one another, they still win.

This is the exact reason why I don't show my kids' faces on social media because I can see people trying to pick apart what features are Black and which aren't. I've grown up with that my whole life. People still do it to me in the comments section, and I don't want that for them. I've had people go as far as to count how many Black people I've posted on my Instagram. Girl, bye! Don't you have a job? That is some long-winded shit right there. Who's got the time to take the tally?

And since you care about me so much, did you also take time to buy my album #ShutUp available on iTunes? Huney, I'm just a big-tittied, freckled-faced bish who loves rosé and hummus, trying to live her life because life is short.

Dark or light, every job that I've had, whether it's in the arts or corporate, if there's another Black girl, people will call us each other's names. No matter how different she looks! It's so crazy that people don't make the effort to learn the Black girls' names: they're just the same person. Every single job this has happened to me. My good friend, hilarious comedian, actress, and host Nicole Byer is a beautiful-ass bish. People think we look alike all the time. It has been happening since 2012. I was in a meeting with a top executive and he said "I love your work on *Nailed It*." Bro, that's not me. That's the other one.

The hair. Oh, the hair. Black women are constantly under scrutiny for every little thing, and it's fucking exhausting. Especially our hair. I was playing a professional woman in a movie and my hair was curly per usual, and I looked presentable. I looked like the bank teller that's good at math and can provide the override when necessary. But it's still me, so yeah, I also looked like the bank teller that's gonna eat all the red lollipops. (I like visuals and Blackstory, sue meh.) One of the producers on the film (a white dude, duh) stopped filming and had beef with the hair people on set. He said, "She's a professional, why is her hair curly?"

Oh Lawd. Here we go. Now he's putting me in a position where I want to bring that caged-animal energy to set like *I thought we were cool and I could trust you, but now look at us.* You clearly don't understand how life works, and I'm gonna have to read you but spin it like I'm not reading you, giving you a life lesson á la sneaking the vegetables into the kids dinner. And I'm really glad this happened to me when I'm older cause younger Michelle wouldn't have handled it so well.

> *Older Michelle: Can we talk real quick in a private room, so not to do this in front of everyone?*
>
> *Younger Michelle: What the fuck did you say about me, muthafucka?*
>
> *Older Michelle: I think it's important that you realize that Black people wear their natural hair and hold many executive positions.*
>
> *Younger Michelle: I cannot believe you came for a bitch like this.*
>
> *Older Michelle: I can't speak for you or anyone else on set, but as the only Black woman in the cast and crew, the fact that you want me to straighten my hair could easily be misunderstood that Black hair is not professional and therefore not good enough, that Black women couldn't possibly be in a position of power unless they looked more white. I don't think that's a very positive message. Do you?*

Younger Michelle: You really wanna go there and fuck with me and my hair, right? Shit. You'll see, you'll fucking see, I'mma call my manager right now; I'mma call Al Sharpton while I'm at it and put a muthafucka on blast, 'cause this shit ain't right.

I saw the lights go on on another producer's face, and she quickly quipped, "Oh, no, no, no, no, this is great. We love your curly hair, and you should wear it as such. It's got so much personality!"

Hmm, *personality*. In the words of the great Nene Leakes: "Okay, I see you. You see me. We each other." I went back to set and filmed the damn thing. After we wrapped, those same producers sent me a five hundred dollar certificate to get a massage at a very fancy place. I swear they should have included a note that read, "Hey, thanks for not calling the ACLU!"

UNITED NATIONS RELATIONS

When it comes to relationships, LOL, I mean random hookups (who are we kidding?), I'm an equal-opportunity heaux. I'm down with the rainbow. Down with people that make me feel good, happy, positive. I'm down with learning about new cultures and their body parts. African American, African, European, Arabic, Jewish, Spanish, Caribbean, South Korean—yes, bitch, these hot-ASS South Korean men are just walking around here with their defined jaws and thunder thighs and you're just sleeping on it?! And all these relationships would be considered interracial. I'm not making up the rules, I'm just trying to pay my taxes on time and get some cardio in a couple of times a week.

Tell you what really pissed people off. A light-skinned bitch married to a white guy. Seems we're still in Virginia in the fifties and my last name is Loving. I've had (what I thought were) friends say some shit about me "thinking I'm 'all that' and that's why I'm with a white dude!" No, bitch. I fell in love with the person that got me the most and he happened to be a white dude from Holland. I wish there was more to it than that, but I'm a simple bitch, and there's all that is. I've heard people throw in the word *fetish* quite a bit when it comes to interracial relationships, and to be honest, I like to keep things neutral, but I'm gonna go ahead and make that blanket of all blanket statements and say that fetishes are mostly a male thing. I don't know any women out here with fetishes. They're trying to keep a clean home, a certain amount of commas in the bank account while maintaining good knees. Women don't have the luxury of time to think about what super specific type of person is gonna give them a lady boner. They're just like, *What the fuck can you add to my life that I need?*

WHEN IN ROME, SAY SOME RACIST SHIT

Traveling really is the best education for every bitch. I thought America held the monopoly on weird, inappropriate remarks and questions for light-skinned folk. But it only took a few international flights to show me the world is a bigger place full of small-minded people. To experience the racism and misogyny for another culture only speaks to how much work we have as humans to get the fuck over whatever seed of dumb, dumb shit was implemented generations ago.

My father used to work in Venezuela. When I'd visit, people would butt me in line, bartenders would ignore me, old men would say weird shit in Spanish I couldn't understand. I asked a friend what one guy said: "Come over here, you fat Brazilian bitch, I'll eat you like the pork chop you are." What in the natural fuck?

In Paris with my friends one time, we all went out dancing at a lounge-type place. My friend Amanda, who's a very sweet, quiet little blond girl, was asked to dance by this older Arabic dude. She didn't want to, told him no a few times, but he refused and held her by her wrists and was dancing with her while she was trying to get loose. And here's something I learned: crazy doesn't have a color. There's an assumption because you're light-skinned that you're supposed to be more proper. I'm a crazy bitch. Don't let the freckles fool you. I stuck up for my girl and let him know she didn't wanna dance. He wasn't trying to hear that. I told him to let her go. In French. In English. With my face. He and I got into it Jerry Springer–style as I peeled his hands off her tiny porcelain ones to keep her from being *Taken 4*. Then he threw wine in my face and said I needed to be a better Egyptian woman and that I was disrespectful.

Another time in a Moroccan neighborhood in Amsterdam a few veiled women mumbled "Fallen Muslim girl" under their breath. And what I've realized is that I've been through a mental and emotional minefield of fuckery finding myself carrying the vintage grudge of ignorance. Whatever race; creed; light-, medium-, dark-skinned; the world will always be hardest on women. That's a connection we have that overshadows any culture. Leave us alone. We're tired.

This isn't just me complaining about how people have treated me. People will always say dumb-ass shit to you no matter how you look. My heart aches for my children because I know people will be rude, hurtful, and just plain ignorant. To be picked apart and scrutinized no matter what color or size you are has long-lasting, damaging effects, and I don't think people realize it. I want to be there to protect them. I want to be on the schoolyard during the dodgeball game and set people straight when something comes out their mouth. When a friend's mom says something so rude you can't even see straight, I want to be there. The need to protect these littles at any and all costs is now my nationality. I know I can't do that forever. No matter what race, culture, or political affiliation, why can't our platform just be kindness? I really wish for my daughter to be confident in who she is, not to believe people when they say she's too this, or not enough that. I want for my son to have his own definition of what a man is. I want my twinsies to know that they are smart, considerate, and independent enough to trust their own decisions. No matter who you decide to be with, or what you do in life, you are enough. You are always enough.

ADVICE YOU CAN FIT ON A MAGNET

Life is a house full of problems. Which room can you live in the longest?

Girl, bye! Everyone and everything, everywhere, will come with some drama. Pick the lesser of two evils before it sucks the calcium out of your body.

Open your mind, your heart, and your legs.

Enough with all the rules when it comes to dating! I met my husband through a one-night stand. You've gotta put yourself out there and let love live! No one plays the lotto once! Jump on it!

Don't tell yourself no before other people tell you no.

Shit doesn't have to be perfect; it just has to be done.

You deserve it.

It's okay if you want someone to pay. It doesn't mean you need them, it just means you're worth it. Don't be so damn independent that you don't know how to receive love.

Fucking practice.

Who the fuck are these people just showing up and winging shit? Have some respect.

If they don't want to hear from you, let them hear about you.

This goes for work, for love, et al. Just keep doing you and love will follow.

It's biology, bitch.

This one is mainly for the ladies; sorry, boo. LADIES: Next time you hear yourself talking to a friend about someone you're dating, not dating, trying to debunk a text message or email, leave that shit alone. Take it out with the recycling twice a week. Don't waste your precious time. Sure, life is short, but also, you ain't gonna be wet forever. It's biology, bitch.

UPGRADE, BITCH.

The time for next level is NOW! Treat ya'self, you deserve it!

Be brave and wear condoms.

You too cute for bacteria.

Self-Care is not selfish.

Say it with me now. Don't be a fucking hero. Put whatever is stressing you out down, walk away, and go get them shoulders rubbed.

Keep it moving.

You've tried to make a relationship work, but it's not going anywhere and you're not happy; how you gonna just keep putting your face in someone's crotch that doesn't wanna better themselves? Keep. It. Moving.

Bye, bish.

Know when to leave a dinner party, when a conversation at a party is over, and when a meeting is done. Yes, your time is valuable, and so is everyone else's.

You are worthy. You are perfect. You are amazing.

Rinse and repeat.

ACKNOWLEDGMENTS

Oh Jesus, acknowledgments are like the last hour of the Oscars—why are you still here? You've already lived through all of this mess, do you really wanna hang out for this? Welp, okay! Here goes, huney . . .

Those teachers, professors, producers, casting peeps, and family members who have told me that they don't think I have it. Thank you. No really, thank you. You've made me tougher, stronger, and realize that if something is important to you, it's worth the fight.

The Dutchie aka Holland Tunnel aka Hice aka Ice aka B-o-b. This dude practically threw me in a room and was all, "We can take care of ourselves stop worrying about us and also what would you like me to make you so you can eat and work." OMG THANK YOU for taking care of me like I was a sassy freckle-face Paul Sheldon in *Misery*. What a love. What a life.

My friends, my chosen family! I've talked their ears off, they've talked off mine. We've celebrated, we've fought, we've ugly-cried, we've done all the things. Franchesca, Giulia, Jordan, Dan, Veronica, Marianne, Rebecca, Eric, Rasheem, Terri, Jen, Jessica, Alison, Ilana, Robert, Falon, Latisha, and Cynthia. Thank you for always picking up the phone.

My manager, Anne Hong. I met her the same year I met Husband and I'm always thankful for these Virgos looking out for me. I'm so glad I've forced you into friendship.

My A-team at CAA and UTA, Rachel, Adam, Erica, Sam, and Mark. Y'all are like cool-ass parents who are all "I love your ideas! You can do anything!" Thank you so much for having my back.

In 2015, Phoebe Robinson introduced me to Robert Guinsler, her book agent. Phoebe was all, "Why can't we write books? We can do anything; work with him!" Thank you, Phoebe, for believing it's all possible and that female empowerment and Black Girl Magic are necessary. And wow, *Robert the Book Agent Guy* was so patient. I was going through so much life shit. I didn't know how to say yes, how to say no, how to finish anything, but he always insisted that I could write this book. Thank you, bish, for championing these titties.

Wow. The peeps at Simon & Schuster. Why did you trust me to write this book?! Who are you people and how did you get such vision?!? I can't deal. THANK YOU Jeremie Ruby-Strauss, Andrew Nguyen, Caroline Pallotta, John Paul Jones, Kayley Hoffman, Kathryn Barrett, Michael Kwan, Erica Ferguson, John Vairo, Lisa Litwack, Sydney Morris,

Abby Zidle, Sally Marvin, Aimee Bell, Jennifer Long, and Jennifer Bergstrom. Team work makes the dream work.

My parents, Michel and Marie, I love you more than life itself. (I hope you skipped the heaux stuff.)

My children, Hazel and Otis, I'm so glad we finally got to meet each other. I love you more than I could ever say.